AMERICAN ESSAYS IN LITURGY

SERIES EDITOR, EDWARD FOLEY

Let Justice Sing
Hymnody and Justice

Paul Westermeyer

A Liturgical Press Book

THE LITURGICAL PRESS
Collegeville, Minnesota

The author has made serious effort to acquire permission where necessary to reprint in this volume copyrighted material of the authors or publishers listed below:

Brian Wren, "If Every naming of God," Crossroad Publishing Company.
Bret Hesla, the hymn beginning "Working hard to survive," titled "Everything That We Have," Augsburg Fortress.

Thomas Troeger, "The Love That Lifted Lyric Praise," from *Borrowed Light,* © 1994 Oxford University Press. Used by permission.

1 2 3 4 5 6 7 8 9

Library of Congress Cataloging-in-Publication Data

Westermeyer, Paul, 1940–
 Let justice sing : hymnody and justice / Paul Westermeyer.
   p. cm. — (American essays in liturgy)
 Includes bibliographical references.
 ISBN 0-8146-2505-3 (alk. paper)
 1. Christianity and justice—History of doctrines. 2. Hymns, English—United States—History and criticism. 3. Hymns, English—History and criticism. 4. Hymns—History and criticism.
I. Title. II. Series: American essays in liturgy (Collegeville, Minn.)
BR115.J8W47 1998
264'.23—dc21
                   98-19837
                    CIP

With grateful appreciation to
Lancaster Seminary and
two compelling Lancaster Seminary teachers:
Gabriel Fackre, who clearly systematized
and perceptively probed theology and ethics with us,
and
Bard Thompson, *in memoriam,* who spread out
the church's history for us
and organically related it to our responsibilities,
and
a fellow Lancaster Seminary graduate,
Francis Williamson, to whom I am indebted
for remarkable, challenging, and invaluable conversations
about hymnody and church music since Seminary days.

Contents

Abbreviations

BH	*The Baptist Hymnal*, 1991
EH	*The [Episcopal] Hymnal*, 1982, 1985
EH1940	*The Hymnal of the Protestant Episcopal Church in the United States of America 1940*
HC	*The Hymnal 1982 Companion* (Glover)
LAAS	*Lyrics of the Afro-American Spiritual*
LBW	*Lutheran Book of Worship*, 1978
LMGM	*Lead Me, Guide Me: The African American Catholic Hymnal*
PH	*The Presbyterian Hymnal*, 1990
RL	*Rejoice in the Lord*, 1985
SBH	*Service Book and Hymnal of the Lutheran Church in America*
UMH	*The United Methodist Hymnal*, 1989
Wor3	*Worship Third Edition*, 1986

Introduction

The theme of the Worship and Music Conference at Montreat in June of 1995 was, "Worship: What Does the Lord Require? Doing Worship . . . Doing Justice." My assignment as the Routley Hymnology Lecturer was to deliver five lectures about hymnody informed by the conference theme.

The relationship of hymnody and justice is a topic I have often thought about but have never sought to systematize. In doing some research about it, I thought I could organize it systematically into five discrete lectures. When I started to write, the material took on a life of its own. I followed where it led. It led neither to the systematic treatment I anticipated nor to five separate lectures but flowed into an extended essay that probed the topic and eventually settled into five chapters. The essay begins with the realization that justice has been a particular concern of recent hymn writers, asks what Christians in the past have sung, and then moves to more general considerations. Its theme is that Christians have always sung about justice, and that the message transcends the messengers. For those who want to chase down the details in specific hymnic repertoires, chapters 2 and 3 are necessary. For those who want to get the broad context and omit the details, chapters 2 and 3 can be omitted or read last.

This is submitted to the church and others who wish to join the moral deliberation it presumes in the form of an open-ended and ongoing discussion, with the hope that it helps us know something more about our past that can be applied with wisdom to our present. I hope it stimulates other studies and a healthy dialogue.

I am grateful to Luther Seminary for sabbatical time to revise and complete this project, and to Robert Brusic, Susan Cherwien,

Gabriel Fackre, Robert Hausman, Michael Hawn, Diane Jacobson, Austin Lovelace, Martin E. Marty, Doris Moye, David Partington, Sandi Shrewsbury, W. Thomas Smith, Brian Wren, Francis Williamson, and Nicholas Wolterstorff for their responses to various drafts of this book. Melva Costen provided insights at Montreat as I was writing and lecturing. Edward Foley, the editor of this series, made perceptive and helpful suggestions. None of these persons is in any way responsible for what I finally chose to say, but their aid as dialogical partners and critics enabled me to think this out far more carefully than I could have done alone.

1 Content: The Twentieth Century

"Dey allus done tell us it am wrong to lie and steal," exploded Josephine Howard of Texas, "but why did white folks steal my mammy and her mammy?"[1]

Josephine Howard was raising many questions in that brief explosion. One of them concerns justice.

With the dead and the dying heaped upon one another in a shed in the dark night of the Holocaust,

> I heard the sound of a violin. . . . It must have been Juliek. . . . He played a fragment from Beethoven's concerto. . . . I had never heard sounds so pure. In such silence.[2]

The sounds of that violin were about many things. One of them concerns justice.

Themes of Justice

Hymn Writers

Late-twentieth-century English hymn writing, often called the hymn explosion, is saturated with the theme of justice. Albert Bayly's "What Does the Lord Require"[3] is an obvious example, as is Erik

---

[1] Genovese, *Roll, Jordan, Roll*, 605.

[2] *Night*, 97–98.

[3] *The [Episcopal] Hymnal 1982*, hereafter *EH*, no. 605; *The Presbyterian Hymnal*, hereafter *PH*, no. 405; *Rejoice in the Lord*, hereafter *RL*, no. 176; *The*

Routley's "All Who Love and Serve Your City"[4] or Joy F. Patterson's "Isaiah the Prophet Has Written of Old."[5] Justice is there when the first line may lead you not to expect it, in hymns like Erik Routley's "New Songs of Celebration Render,"[6] which has us singing of God's truth and righteousness by the end of the first stanza and of our just God who establishes peace by the end of the third.

Some writers, like Brian Wren, have gone after justice with a passion. "Thank You, God, for Water, Soil, and Air"[7] is a confession of our ecological recklessness and a prayer that we may act justly on behalf of others. Wren is not only concerned about ecology. He has challenged the church to do justice at many points, one of which is the way we use language both for humanity and for God in our hymnody. "Dear Sister God"[8] illustrates that concern in one of his hymns, but Wren has also thought out the topic at book length in *What Language Shall I Borrow?*[9] There, in poetic fashion, he articulates "The Main Question" like this:

> If
> *every naming of God*
> *is a borrowing from human experience*
> And if
> *language slants and angles*
> *our thinking and behavior,*
> And if
> *our society*
> *makes qualities labeled "feminine"*
> *inferior to qualities labeled "masculine,"*
> *forming men and women*
> *with identities steeped in those labelings,*
> *in structures where men are still dominant though shaken*
> *and women still subordinate though seeking emancipation . . .*

United Methodist Hymnal, hereafter *UMH,* no. 441; *Worship Third Edition: A Hymnal and Service Book for Roman Catholics,* hereafter *Wor3,* no. 625.

[4] *EH,* 570, 571; *Lutheran Book of Worship,* hereafter *LBW,* no. 436; *PH,* no. 413; *RL,* no. 485; *UMH,* no. 433; *Wor3,* no. 621.

[5] *PH,* no. 337.

[6] *EH,* no. 413; *PH,* no. 218; *RL,* no. 119; *Wor3,* no. 533.

[7] *PH,* no. 266; *RL* no. 22.

[8] Brian Wren, *Faith Looking Forward,* no. 3.

[9] Brian Wren, *What Language Shall I Borrow?*

Then it follows that
using only male language
("he," "king," "father")
to name and praise God
powerfully affects our encounter with God
and our thinking and behavior;

So that we must then ask
whether male dominance and female subordination
and seeing God only in male terms
are God's intention
or human distortion and sin;

For if
these things are indeed
a deep distortion and sin,
So that
women and men are called to repent together
from domination and subordination,

Then how
can we name and praise God
in ways less idolatrous,
more freeing,
and more true
to the Triune God
and the direction of love
in the Anointed One, Jesus?[10]

Clearly for Brian Wren matters of justice are not some accretion that got accidentally joined to texts of hymns. He has devoted considerable time and effort to sorting out such issues in a careful and orderly process of thought,[11] and he has attempted to embody them in his hymn writing.

Fred Kaan exhibits some of this same self-conscious passion for justice in his thoughts about hymn writing[12] and in his hymns too, as, for example, "Help Us Accept Each Other."[13] Thomas Troeger

[10] Ibid., 1–2.
[11] For further sorting by Brian Wren, see his *Education for Justice*.
[12] For Kaan's comments and those of other twentieth-century hymn writers see Paul Westermeyer, *With Tongues of Fire*.
[13] *UMH*, no. 560; *PH*, no. 358; *Wor3*, no. 656.

has also carefully thought this out[14] and has woven themes of justice into the words with which he has crafted the Biblical materials. "The Least in God's Kingdom Is Greater Than John," "The Love That Lifted Lyric Praise," and "Too Splendid for Speech but Ripe for a Song" are foremost illustrations.[15]

Themes of justice are also there in the hymns of hymn writers from our period who are less self-conscious about them. In Martin Franzmann's "O God, O Lord of Heaven and Earth,"[16] when you have sung through "our poisoned air" and "deep despair" and get to a "life of praise," justice is clearly part of such a life. Glorifying God leads Fred Pratt Green to move each stanza of "When in Our Music God Is Glorified"[17] to "Alleluia," but that brings with it "no room for pride" in the first stanza and truth "in liturgy and song" against "centuries of wrong" in the third, so that justice is inescapable there too. The theme takes over the whole of Pratt Green's "The Church of Christ in Every Age,"[18] as "victims of injustice cry for shelter and for bread to eat" and the singing church acknowledges its responsibility as servants "clothed in Christ's humanity." Examples from other hymn writers could be multiplied.

Communities and Groups

Communities and groups among us also exhibit these concerns. The *Wild Goose Songs*[19] created by John Bell and the Iona Community in Scotland are shot through with themes of justice. "Blessed Are You Poor," a setting of the Beatitudes, is just one example among many that could be cited.[20]

Folk-like groups whose hymnic and musical doing is driven in whole or part by concerns for justice have sprung up in many places. Bread for the Journey in Minneapolis, with Mary Preus, Tom Witt, and other musicians, is a good example. This group utilizes a vari-

---

[14] See Westermeyer, *With Tongues of Fire,* pp. 131–132, 133–134.

[15] Troeger, *Borrowed Light,* nos. 112, 47, 48.

[16] *LBW,* no. 396.

[17] *The Baptist Hymnal,* hereafter *BH,* no. 435; *EH,* no. 420; *LBW,* 555; *UMH,* no. 68; *PH,* no. 264; *RL,* no. 508; *Wor3,* no. 549.

[18] *BH,* no. 402; *UMH,* no. 589; *LBW,* no. 433; *PH,* no. 421; *Wor3,* no. 626.

[19] Bell and Maule, *Heaven Shall Not Wait;* idem, *Enemy of Apathy;* idem, *Love from Below.*

[20] Bell and Maule, *Love from Below,* 48.

ety of texts and musical styles from many cultures and produces songbooks called *Sing a New Song,* which collate these materials for congregational use. The presence of materials from different cultures contains its own message of justice, but the texts such groups generate on their own also embody that message, often in a rough way that flaunts traditional hymnic disciplines with the naive fury of the anchoritic monk. Here's an example by Bret Hesla, included in one edition of *Sing a New Song.*

> Working hard to survive is no guarantee.
> The deck is always stacked against the poor.
> If we'd use just what we need,
> Reject the creeping cancer of greed,
> Like a miracle the hungry would be fed.
>
> Holding on to the past, to the times that have gone
> Can only rob the present of its joy.
> And if we cling to our gold
> So that the future is secure,
> We have robbed the poor while chasing a mirage.
>
> May we show gratitude in the way that we live
> And not with pompous prayers and fancy feasts.
> Let go of ease as our goal,
> And work to make creation whole.
> That's the offering that God is asking for.[21]

Hymnals and Hymnal Committees

Committees that have produced denominational hymnals in our period have struggled with justice in their editing. Weaving in materials from many cultures is one way they have sought to do that. It has not been as easy for them as it has been for ad hoc groups because they have the inertia of their denomination's heritage and memory to contend with. But it has been part of their concern, and they have often successfully included many pieces outside their own traditions.[22]

---

[21] *Sing a New Song,* 46.
[22] *Hymnal, A Worship Book, Prepared by Churches in the Believers Church Tradition* is one of the most obvious illustrations.

One of their chief struggles has concerned language both for humanity and for God. Most hymnal committees have been able to come to some clarity about human language: generic male pronouns are no longer possible, nor is language that discriminates against a group of people—"washing us white" against "blacks," for example. Language about God is far more complex, and solutions have been more perplexing.

Decisions about what language to use have concerned more than gender. Many other uses have been viewed as more or less dangerous and discriminatory: militaristic language, dark/white contrasts, and images that make disabled people feel less than human. Concerns about a pre-Copernican three-story universe may turn out to be important as well, but they have received comparatively little attention and are not so related to the topic of this book.[23] Throughout this process most responsible hymnal committees have tried to respect the church's memory bank and at the same time use language that is not discriminatory, oppressive, or androcentric.[24] The task has not been easy. Agreements or solutions that seem momentarily to work have often evaporated after a short time has passed. Any editing, no matter how necessary, how skillful, how well intentioned, and how positive, almost always involves some loss,[25] which may not be evident to those who do the editing. Problems are always more evident to generations that follow.

Whether hymnal committees have always succeeded, or what one may think about their solutions, is not the point. The point here is that they have struggled. The theme of justice has been front and center time and time again in our period.

---

[23] *The New Century Hymnal* is an exception. Its editors altered most texts in common usage, seeking to avoid up/down language as well as what was regarded as discriminatory and non-inclusive for humanity and for God. Whether the thoroughgoing sameness of this revision and its (unjust?) disregard for the memory bank of the Christian church will yield unintentional theological and poetic sleepers, ultimately reversing what the editors intended, remains to be seen with usage or its absence. *Cf.* Madeleine Forell Marshall, "The Holy Ghost Is Amorous in His Metaphors," 17–23; Young, "The New Century Hymnal, 1995," 25–38.

[24] For overviews of issues related to language see Ramshaw, *God Beyond Gender*; Fackre, "Ways of Inclusivity," 52–65.

[25] Robin Leaver points this out in the editing that has been done to Martin Franzmann's hymns. See Leaver, *Come to the Feast.*

Justice and Twentieth-Century Christians

That justice should concern Christians is not surprising. One can't read the Bible very long without realizing that justice is a central concern in it. As Nicholas Wolterstorff points out, God cares about justice because God cares for the little one, the outcast. We are commanded to do likewise, to be icons of God who identify with the weak and defenseless. To be the holy people of a holy God demands doing justice, because injustice is unholy. In Christ the "coming of full-orbed shalom, the arrival of holiness upon earth," has broken in, and the church as Christ's body on earth is to continue struggling for justice.[26]

For some Christians in our century justice has become an especially important and intense focus in ways that are far broader than the hymnic ones. Concerns for justice in hymnody are but manifestations of a deeper cultural struggle, symbolized in the quotations with which this chapter began. We have lived through two world wars; experienced a Holocaust against the Jews and a nuclear firestorm in Hiroshima and Nagasaki; seen the slaughter of countless innocent people—many children among them; struggled for racial justice in the United States after slavery; sought to rectify past wrongs for native Americans; witnessed South Africa, Vietnam, Northern Ireland, Iran, Israel, Bosnia, Croatia, etc., and all the killing and destruction associated with those places; fought for the equality of women; agonized about nuclear storage; tried to figure out how the have-nots of the world could possess their share of the world's abundance and how the haves would not treat the world's abundance as their possession or see themselves as gatekeepers for the have-nots; sought to do something positive about the despoiling of our environment; tried to eliminate unjust discrimination against homosexuals; worked at laws that would not discriminate against anybody or any group of people; too often worked against justice and confessed our injustice in all these matters; and realized how interconnected and complex our "global village" is.

Some might say the sixteenth century was concerned about how to find a gracious God, while we of the twentieth century are concerned about how to find a gracious neighbor or how to organize a gracious neighborhood. Such a comparison may or may not be precisely accurate. After all, every generation has had to figure out how

---

[26] Wolterstorff, "Why Care About Justice?" 156–67.

to live together in some neighborly fashion, and we are not the first people who have faced horrible situations. People in different periods of history do have different vocations, however, and the church discovers more fully and works out more completely different pieces and implications of the Christian message in different times and places. The fourth century had to work out christological and trinitarian questions, the sixteenth focused on justification, and the nineteenth on confessional, liturgical, and eucharistic matters. A central part of our vocation in the twentieth century has been seeking justice and exploring its ramifications. All periods, to be sure, have had all the concerns to deal with, which is why we are still dealing with them all today. Christological and trinitarian questions, for example, still engage us deeply.[27] But certain themes seem to have been more pressing at different periods, and justice is certainly one of ours.

Justice

What does "justice" mean? The dictionary defines it as "moral rightness, equity, fairness." If you look up "Justice" in *The Interpreter's Dictionary of the Bible,* you are sent to "Law; Righteousness; Peace in the O[ld] T[estament]."[28] "Law" leads to the Ten Commandments,[29] "Righteousness" requires a discussion of relationships with God and the neighbor,[30] and "Peace in the OT" is defined as "the state of wholeness possessed by persons or groups, which may be health, prosperity, security, or the spiritual completeness of covenant."[31] James White defines justice as "attributing to all persons their full human worth, *i.e.,* rendering to each person what is due that person as a human being." He quotes Aquinas' definition as "a habit whereby man [sic] renders to each one his due by a constant and perpetual will."[32]

---

[27] For some of this discussion—here Trinity and justice specifically in relation to hymnody—see Wren, *What Language Shall I Borrow?* 195–214.

[28] Buttrick, *Interpreter's Dictionary of the Bible,* E-J, 1027.

[29] Ibid., K–Q, 80ff.

[30] Ibid., R–Z, 80ff.

[31] Ibid., K–Q, 704.

[32] James F. White, "Worship as a Source of Injustice," 72. Cf. Wren, *Education for Justice,* 32: "The basic idea of justice is giving people their due, what they deserve or ought to have."

These brief definitions give a sense of the breadth of the meaning of justice, which biblical scholars, systematic theologians, and ethicists explore in far more detail than is possible here.[33] Any time morality, ethics, equity, fairness, the law, righteousness, peace, human worth, or similar matters are called into play, themes of justice are there. Justice has to do with relationships between human beings and between God and human beings.

Is there some way to order the breadth that is present here? I think so. At the risk of oversimplification, it would seem possible to say that justice *at the human level* involves two basic areas. One is right relations, which we act out one to one with those who are there next to us (our neighbors), and the other is right relations in the society as a whole and, indeed, to the whole creation, where broader systemic nets that we can't see so easily encompass and in some measure control us. For the Christian both areas fall under *God*, whose Trinity of being is itself a relationship of justice, and under God's intention for us to live in peaceful, ethically whole relationships with others.

The individual relations of this fabric are easier to comprehend, though not necessarily easier to do. Finding someone beaten on the side of the road requires that I stop, bind up the person's wounds, and then find a hospital if necessary. I may resist doing that, but the action required is clear and straightforward. This action may be called compassion or kindness or ethical response as distinct from a narrower definition of justice, but it is justice in the sense of White's and Aquinas' descriptions, namely, giving to other people their "due," their full human worth. It can be divorced from systemic issues, so that kindness can operate within a system of injustice like apartheid, but then something is terribly wrong and the intrinsic fullness and implications of the ethical response have been denied. At some point the full implications invariably come into view.

Things get more complicated when the presence of systemic issues become apparent. What if the person who appears to be beaten by the side of the road is actually a setup, so that I will be robbed by co-conspirators when I stop to help? And what about antecedent causes in my society that produce or at least create the climate for

---

[33] For an introduction to the complexity of the topic see Tillich, *Love, Power, and Justice*, where he argues one has to see these realities in the light of humanity's being and of being-itself.

robbers in the first place? What should I do about that in order to live justly? The action required here may be more closely related to what we normally define as justice.

Challenging injustice at the level of societal structures is very difficult. What does one do to alter a system that discriminates unjustly against African Americans? When does one do it? Some moments seem ripe, and some don't. Why did Rosa Parks' refusal to move from her seat on a bus in Montgomery, Alabama, ignite a movement when not too many years earlier such an action might have prompted an unreported death? What part did all the past unreported deaths and the courageous actions behind them play in the movement Rosa Parks' action began? In hindsight one can say relatively easily that Martin Luther King, Jr., accomplished much for justice and made many right choices, but living history the way we have to live it, namely, forward, is not so easy. He had to make decisions in the face of criticism without knowing how things would come out and knowing that there had been people before him who had not managed to change anything.[34] Perhaps the time was "ripe" in our age, which points again to seeking justice as one of our vocations.

So far we've discussed justice as a human matter. But for the Christian it is *not simply a human matter.* It is not only about human relationships, individual or systemic, and trying to do something about those relationships. It is far broader than that. It has to do with *the living God and with God in Christ.* Is God just? Is there a God of justice at all? In an ambiguous and evil world that is unjust no matter what we do, where human justice itself is undermined by a cancerous net from which there is no escape, by complexity, and by all sorts of clever obfuscations, can one even know what it is? Are there any benchmarks at all? What does God in Christ have to do with this?

The Christian confession is that we are engaged by a living God known in Christ through the Spirit. We cannot escape that God anywhere—in the highest heaven or the depths of the sea or the darkest night or the brightest day.[35] Like it or not, that creator God is a God of justice, there to bless and judge. Like it or not, the benchmarks of treating one another justly are there for all humanity to see and figure out, we are called to do justly, and we choose

[34] King penned his *Letter from Birmingham Jail,* in response to clergy who called his actions "unwise and untimely," 3.

[35] See Psalm 139.

not to do it. Like it or not, there is a rift that separates humanity from God. In Christ, says the Christian, that rift is healed, the battle is won, atonement with God is made, justice is done, mercy is given. That last outrageous assertion is at once both incredibly simple and amazingly complex. At its simplest or most complex, it is a theological statement that points beyond itself to mystery. Theology here, as inevitably for the Christian, becomes doxology.[36] As Francis Williamson puts it, "The goal of human life is love and praise, wonder in the presence of the Triune God—which is the most important contribution the various churches bring to the struggle for justice."[37] Or, in the words of Harmon Smith, cast in terms of the moral life,

> Christians are a people whose vision of the moral life is formed by adoration and praise, by penitence and pardon, by thanksgiving and offering, by revelation and confession . . . and by all of these ascribed and supplicated to the God whom we know through Jesus. When our vision of the moral life is formed in these ways, we Christians will know that we worry about war and sexuality and racism and the rest [including justice] *soli Deo gloria*.[38]

It is possible to organize the breadth of justice systematically in some way as I have just done. But hymnody is not systematic theology. It operates at the level of poetry and metaphor, where ideas run into one another and suggest, presume, or link up with each other. In hymnody, therefore, the breadth of any topic gets swampier than I have just described. The breadth does not yield the neat and careful categories that some may wish. As will become obvious, my point will be that justice is (to change the metaphor) part of the warp and woof of this breadth. We may miss it or avoid it because of our blindness or curved-inwardness. But over time it will break into our consciousness. In hymnody the breadth has to be considered.

I am not suggesting here that hymnody exhibits lack of care or that it is confusing, imprecise, avoids theological integrity, or makes affirmations that deny central Christian theological tenets. Hymns may do those things, but then they have short lives or are used for

---

[36] For eschatology as the way to get at this see Saliers, *Worship as Theology*.
[37] Personal correspondence from Francis Williamson, September 13, 1995.
[38] Smith, *Where Two or Three Are Gathered*, 2–3.

other reasons than their clarity. My point is just the reverse, namely, that the nature of precision, care, and integrity in the church's hymnody is not that of systematic theology. Hymnody pieces together the church's central affirmations in poetic imagery that, as Madeleine Marshall reminds us, actually means something.[39] But it finally issues in doxology, not systematic logic. One is not better than the other. We need both. Each feeds the other.

Can We Sing It?

One might wonder if what has just been said about justice gets into matters beyond the scope of hymnody. Yes, in the sense that ethicists and systematicians have made far more linear and logical sense of these matters at far greater length than is possible for hymn writers. These matters do relate to hymnody, however, because they raise a fundamental question: does justice sing? Given the complications and ambiguities of understanding and doing justice, how can we sing about it at all? Can we sing about it in some authentic way? Is singing about it either pompous and inauthentic self-flagellation when we are or think we are unjust, or is it a self-congratulatory activity by which we who sing think we are just and on God's side? Do we avoid the actual doing of justice by substituting a false type of worship for it?[40] Can one avoid the dilemma?

On the face of it, Amos 5:21-24 might suggest that singing about justice is not possible, certainly not at a time of disobedient injustice. "I hate, I despise your . . . solemn assemblies," Amos says on behalf of God.

> Take away from me the noise
>   of your songs;

---

[39] See Madeleine Forell Marshall, *Common Hymnsense.* One of Marshall's subpoints is especially important, that hymns mean something on their own merits and that the hagiography of the hymn writers is in this sense irrelevant. See pages 9–10.

[40] See the second stanza of Fred Pratt Green, "When the Church of Jesus" (*BH,* no. 396; *UMH,* no. 592):

> If our hearts are lifted where devotion soars
> high above this hungry, suffering world of ours,
> lest our hymns should drug us to forget its needs,
> forge our Christian worship into Christian deeds.

> I will not listen to the melody
>   of your harps.
> But let justice roll down like
>   waters,
> and righteousness like an
>   ever-flowing stream.

The medium here is itself poetic and musical, so that God's rebuke is carried in the very medium it seems to attack. This suggests that Amos is not attacking the song and the worship themselves but their untenable and hypocritical perversions when justice itself is not done. If in fact poetry is the very medium of the prophetic rebuke, then justice can sing and be sung. King David's song in 2 Sam 23:1-7, Randall Thompson's choral setting of it,[41] and Thomas Troeger's hymnic account would seem to suggest that justice not only can sing; it must sing.

> The love that lifted lyric praise
> from David's harp and shepherd soul
> in younger, gladder, golden days
> grew deeper as the king grew old.
> His sweet, clear voice now cracked and thin,
> his hands too stiff to pluck a string,
> he still was stirred by faith within
> to write one final psalm to sing.
>
> He rummaged through his mind for themes
> and stumbled first on early scenes:
> a flock of sheep by quiet streams,
> Goliath and the Philistines,
> the ark brought home, the cheering crowd,
> his rise to honor, wealth and fame—
> and then he thought of deeds less proud,
> of private lust and public shame.
>
> At once the old, repentant king
> discerned the theme of his last song:
> no hero's epic would he sing
> but words of faith, and right and wrong,

---

[41] Randall Thompson, "The Last Words of David," an anthem that is now difficult to use because it was written before concerns about inclusive language but that nonetheless sings very well about justice.

what he had learned from forty years
while holding Zion's troubled throne,
the truth distilled from all the fears
and plots and struggles he had known.

He sang that justice is the rain,
and justice is the ripening sun,
and justice gives the growth and gain
which brutal force has never won.
O listen to that ancient king,
you passing rulers, proud and strong!
Heed David's last psalmed whispering
and live the wisdom of this song.[42]

Maybe the real issue is this. Justice does sing, but the song gets stuck in the throats of the oppressors. Even those who stand idly by and do nothing or have good intent may not sing so easily, or may wind up judging themselves when they do sing too easily.[43] The oppressed, however, sing with mournful and joyful abandon. Witness African American spirituals: "O Mary, don't you weep, don't you mourn; Pharaoh's army got drownded." The oppressor can even learn this song of the oppressed and be liberated. Here is faith in a God of justice who will prevail. To assume "prevail" means some future reward with little relevance to justice in our lives now is a big mistake, for the justice of God not only will prevail above, beyond, and at the end of history, it also sets in motion an engine among the people for right individual and right societal relations here and now. The individual relations will happen quietly, but justice denied in the society will only lead at the "ripe" time to an explosion related to the underlying song. Witness civil rights struggles in our period.

Maybe the real issue is even deeper. The song of justice is implicit in the Christian community's corporate song of praise to God. Justice sings because the song of praise to God is a song of justice. But there are times when we avoid it. Then what is implicit in the corporate song of doxology becomes explicit in the individual prophetic rebuke, and the words of Amos silence our song, which has become hypocritical noise.

---

[42] Troeger, *Borrowed Light*, no. 47.
[43] See Brian Wren's hymn, "Not Only Acts of Evil Will," in Wren, *Piece Together Praise*, 115.

Justice Omitted

While justice has engaged our century's attention, including our hymnody and worship, we have also omitted or avoided it. I have in mind here not only our failure to do justice in the world—a perennial problem of every generation that Christians understand to be part of what is identified by the code word "sin"—but omissions about justice in our worship and its song.

This tendency can be seen whenever the Christian message has been domesticated. For example, many Christmas celebrations in the twentieth century—earlier too—have turned the coming of the holy and just God into "narrowly focused . . . sentimental devotion on Jesus' birth."[44] Only *The [Episcopal] Hymnal 1982* includes this stanza of Phillips Brooks' "O Little Town of Bethlehem." Other hymnals have consistently omitted it.

> Where children pure and happy
>   pray to the blessed Child,
> where misery cries out to thee,
>   Son of the mother mild;
> where charity stands watching
>   and faith holds wide the door,
> the dark night wakes, the glory breaks,
>   and Christmas comes once more.[45]

These words may have been omitted because they have the disadvantage of suggesting that the coming of Christmas is dependent on our doing charity. In the context of the rest of the hymn that interpretation is hard to sustain, however. It is more likely that the uncomfortable prophetic implications of the Christmas message they clearly embody is what has made hymnal committees shy away from including them.

We also omit justice in our hymnody when we take the ethical portion that relates to doing acts of compassion for our neighbor out of the context of the societal and systemic concern for the dispossessed and oppressed. A controlling class can easily do this and not even realize what it has done. That is one reason the church always has to remember to sing the full catholicity of its song. In this case

---

[44] Schattauer, "The Church Year," 36.
[45] *EH*, no. 78.

that means singing the song of the oppressed. Our in-grown curve can even turn this into a form of paternalistic slumming or co-opting the message, but, as Michael Hawn points out,

> There is a delicious paradox that the music of the oppressed (African American spirituals, African, Asian, Latin American, etc.) can become the vehicle for freeing the oppressor. "The truth will make us free." The beauty of justice in song is that the truth grips us and frees us (even to move and dance) before we know it.[46]

Taking God's Place

Any time we create insulated capsules with which we shut out the world and its needs, especially in our worship, the fire of Amos' prophetic cry burns with pain. We will have to return to this theme with matters that are related not to content but to the context of worship and the musical and visual arts that carry the content. Those matters are more subtle. But there is also one final, subtle concern related to content.

It is this: to put the words of God into the mouth of the congregation without the narrative links to indicate who is speaking. Without the narrative links, as in "Go Down, Moses"[47] or the first stanza's question in "How Firm a Foundation,"[48] the congregation is in danger of thinking in a subconscious or subliminal way that it is God. When Amos speaks words of rebuke to the people on behalf of a righteous and angry God, the distinction between God and the people is unmistakable. Hymns that put God's words into the congregations' mouth, however, blur the distinction and convey the unspoken but strong message that we are God. This message supports much of our century's arrogance and undermines God as righteous judge along with God's call for us to do justice, though I suspect hymn writers who have written such hymns did not intend that. Their motives have no doubt been very good. I have heard Gary Simpson argue that perhaps hymn writers are speaking this way be-

[46] Personal correspondence with Michael Hawn, September 17, 1995.
[47] *EH*, no. 647; *Lead Me, Guide Me*, hereafter *LMGM*, no. 292; *PH*, no. 334; *UMH*, no. 448.
[48] *BH*, no. 338; *EH*, no. 636, 637; *LBW*, no. 508; *LMGM*, no. 102; *UMH*, no. 529; *PH*, no. 361; *RL*, no. 172; *Wor3*, no. 585.

cause preachers have ceased to speak any word from God at all. That is a tempting theory, but I suspect it is wishful thinking. Marty Haugen has done a quick survey and provisionally concluded that no hymns were written like this before the 1960s. That leads me to believe this is one of our generation's versions of the perennial human problem from which none of us can escape and which takes different shapes at different times and places, namely, trying to be God or to put ourselves in the place of God. The effect is that we, not God, define justice.

"Borning Cry"[49] exemplifies this tendency. So does "Go, My Children, with My Blessing,"[50] which in other respects is, as is typical for Jaroslav Vajda, a fine hymn. Two further examples are "This Is My Body" and "I, the Lord of Sea and Sky."[51]

---

[49] *With One Voice*, no. 770.

[50] Ibid., no. 721.

[51] Ibid., nos. 707, 752. The second of these can be seen as either making matters better or worse with the refrain where "I" becomes the people responding to God. The quotation marks in the stanzas or a separate voice or group singing them could be understood to help, whereas everyone singing everything and paying little attention to the structure of the text (not unknown in hymn leading and hymn singing!) could be understood to heighten our identification with God.

2 Content: Before the Twentieth Century, I

Are we the first Christians to sing about justice? That assertion is often made. Is it true? One way to check it out is by analyzing some of the hymns we have inherited from Christians who have gone before us and peeking in here and there at what some of them have sung.[1]

The Psalms

As They Stand in the Bible

The psalms are in the blood of the church, and they are the source of its hymnody. To them the church has returned again and again for renewal both in its public worship life and in its individual members' devotional lives. Psalms have been consistently used by the church in its Sunday eucharistic worship, in its baptismal liturgies, and in its daily prayer; this is true across history and across denominational and confessional lines.[2] Psalms have been

---

[1] There are other repertoires than the ones here that could be studied. For example, Stephen Marini is preparing a database of the three hundred most often republished hymns in approximately two hundred American Protestant hymnals and tunebooks from 1737 to 1950. That group of hymns could be analyzed for themes of justice.

[2] See Lamb, *Psalms in Christian Worship.* A passage attributed to Chrysostom (though spurious, there is no reason to doubt its content), says that in virtually all of the worship of the church "David is first and middle and last." See McKinnon, *Music in Early Christian Literature,* 90.

central in the daily monastic offices of the church for Benedictines and other such groups. Luther worked his hymnody out from the psalms. The Calvinist tradition began with metrical psalms as their center, with canticles, the Apostles' Creed, the Decalogue, and the Lord's Prayer added to them.[3] Numerous poets have written metrical Psalters; Sylvia Dunstan was working on one when she died. The psalms are quoted amply, more often than the gospels apparently,[4] in Thomas à Kempis' *Imitation of Christ*, which has been a classical devotional piece for many Christians. The psalms, or substantial pieces of them, more than any other texts are in the memory bank of Christians, for example, Psalms 1, 23, 84, 90, 121, 139, and 150. This becomes especially obvious to pastors, who themselves use the psalms repeatedly in their pastoral care, particularly at the beds of those who are dying. Composers for the church have set psalm texts more than any others.

The psalms are everywhere in the past and present life of the church. Though in recent times they have not always been sung, their most usual form has been in song. They are at heart poetic/musical creations that settle into an incipient musical flow even when they are read. It is no accident, therefore, that there are so many simple psalm tones, so many tunes for metrical psalms, and so many anthems, motets, and longer musical pieces that utilize psalm texts. Igor Stravinsky's *Symphony of Psalms* is an example of the complex end of the spectrum.

Beginning with the psalms is logical, therefore, in any discussion of hymnody. Is justice one of their ingredients? Anybody who knows the psalms at all knows that the answer is yes, that they are saturated with justice even more than the twentieth century's hymnody.

The words "justice" and "just" themselves appear repeatedly in the psalms (Pss 10:18; 33:5; 37:28; 72:1; 94:15; 103:6; 146:7; 9:4; 119:121; 145:17, etc.),[5] but that only begins to explain this theme in them. To sing the psalms is to know an awesome God of infinite range, inescapable yet distinct from finite humanity and the brief spans of individual people (Pss 139; 90). God loves righteousness and justice (Pss 33:5; 97:2), strikes terror in humanity (Pss 2; 9; 97;

---

[3] See, for example, Doran, "Metrical Psalmody," 60.

[4] See R. E. O. White, *Christian Handbook to the Psalms*, 3–4.

[5] The psalms given throughout this discussion are simply meant as examples. Others could be cited.

99), breaks the teeth of the wicked (Ps 3:7), judges the earth (Pss 98; 110:5-6), but also forgives, pardons, and withdraws wrath and anger (Ps 85:2-3). Human beings have two choices, the just law of the Lord or wickedness (Ps 1). Wickedness is not only a choice; it is out there over against us: the psalmist has many foes (Pss 3:1; 6:7; 30:1; 38:12). These foes are never defined, but they seem to be people who are also in some sense personified forces. Whoever they are, they side with evil and persecute the poor (Ps 10:2). God judges justly, however, and defends the poor, the orphan, the widow, and the humble (Pss 10:18; 41:1-3; 149:4).

Human beings are clearly expected to do the same (Ps 82). Living justly is the business of individuals toward one another (Pss 26; 37:3; 128:1) and of those who take counsel for the people and their society as a whole. Kings therefore pray for God's justice to "judge the people with righteousness and the poor with justice" (Ps 72:1-2). When kings conspire against God, they can expect laughter from the heavens with just fury and wrath kindled against them (Ps 2).

The psalmist cries to God "to defend my cause" (Ps 9:4) and to wake up "for my defense" (Ps 35:23). This remarkably free, honest, and forthright encounter between the psalmist and God can turn from its positive form to a negative whining self-righteousness, but that evaporates very quickly because the psalmist also knows the depth "of my sin" (Pss 38:3; 51:3) and prays that God will "be gracious to me, for I have sinned" (Pss 41:4; 51:2).

Justice is on every page of the Psalter. It is not the only thing there, to be sure. Texts of mercy, lament, praise, rage, petition, and vengeance also abound. Justice nonetheless is central to this great book of wisdom. In Walter Brueggemann's words, Israel's faith and doxology is

> revolutionary in its world-making [and] raw in its power. . . . The nations are invited to a new world with a public ethic rooted in and normed by tales of nameless peasants, widows, and orphans. It is enough to make trees sing and fields clap and floods rejoice and barren women laugh and liberated slaves dance and angels sing.[6]

Israel's vision makes the close association of justice with song not surprising. Not only is justice sung in the very musical medium of

[6] Brueggemann, *Israel's Praise*, 85–86.

the Psalter, but justice leads to song and song to justice in the content of the psalms themselves.

Psalm 67 is a good illustration. In this thanksgiving for God's bounty to us in the harvest from the earth, the prayer is made at the beginning and the end of the psalm that God would continue to bless us. Part of that prayer is for God's way to be known on earth, which leads to the refrain of praise in verse 3. Then comes a petition for the nations to be glad and sing for joy, and immediately, "for you judge the peoples with equity and guide the nations upon earth," followed again by the refrain of praise from verse 3, which is now verse 5. Not only is the whole medium musical, but the very content itself moves back and forth between justice and song.

In Psalm 69 things get a little more vicious, but the same relationship is there. A prayer that justice be done to enemies who falsely accuse and persecute leads to a song of praise and thanksgiving to God, who makes the oppressed glad and hears the needy. Psalm 75 goes the other way. In the Old Testament's typical form of blessing, it begins with a song of thanks, then cites God's wondrous deeds, which include executing judgment. In Psalm 104:35, right after a song of praise comes this, "Let sinners be consumed from the earth, and let the wicked be no more."

Justice is sung throughout the psalms. Justice and song lead back and forth to one another, and the whole Psalter with all its concerns for justice leads to the song of praise in Psalm 150 toward which the whole cosmos is moving.[7] The telos of praise to God contains justice within it as part of its very essence.

In Metrical Versions

THE SEVENTEENTH CENTURY

Tate and Brady. One might ask whether the content of the Psalter that I have just described is maintained for a community that has put all the psalms in metrical forms. Does the move to rhymed paraphrases obliterate the element of justice? To answer such a question would require carefully examining a specific Psalter and its use in a given community. Since Calvinists are the ones who mainly produced metrical Psalters, and since Calvinists were such sticklers for being as literal as possible in their translations of the psalms, one

---

[7] Cf. Miller, "Psalms as Praise and Poetry," 15.

could anticipate the answer to such a question. But to test it out, I went to the library and decided to work through whatever metrical Psalter was available. The one by the Irishmen Nahum Tate (1652–1715), poet laureate under William III, and Nicholas Brady (1659–1726), a royal chaplain, was the first one I found.[8] The Tate and Brady Psalter was accused of not being literal enough when it was published in 1696,[9] so it turns out to be a good one to check. References to justice are there as strongly as ever. Here are some examples.

> According to thy sov'reign Name,
>   Thy praise through earth extends;
> Thy pow'rful arm, as Justice guides,
>   Chastises or defends.
>   (Ps 48:8)[10]

> Mark this, ye wicked fools, lest I
> Let all my bolts of vengeance fly,
>   Whilst none shall dare your cause to own:
> Who praises me, due honour gives;
> And to the man that justly lives
>   My strong salvation shall be shown.
>   (Ps 50:12)[11]

> God in the great assembly stands,
>   Where his impartial eye
> In state surveys the earthly gods,
>   And does their judgments try.
> How dare ye then unjustly judge
>   Or be to sinners kind?
> Defend the orphans and the poor;
>   Let such your justice find.

> Protect the humble helpless man,
>   Reduc'd to deep distress;
> And let not him become a prey
>   To such as would oppress.
>   (Ps 82:1-3)[12]

---

[8] The version I found was N. Tate and N. Brady, *A New Version of the Psalms of David.*

[9] See Doran, "Metrical Psalmody," 65.

[10] Tate and Brady, *A New Version*, 93.

[11] Ibid., 98.

[12] Ibid., 165.

One could say that Tate and Brady feels a bit less gracious than the original prose versions of the psalms and that grace and mercy seem more clothed with fear. This may be because of the weight given to fear or because "decrees" take on a Calvinist hue or because of the formal restrictions in the "steady jog trot" of common meter (which is not true for the Genevan French Psalter with its 110 meters). But justice is certainly not absent from this metrical version of the psalms.

The psalms are laced with justice in their prose and at least in this metrical version. But what if they are not used as a whole? What if they are paraphrased more freely, and only some of them are used?

THE EIGHTEENTH CENTURY

Watts. One obvious place to go with such questions is to the Congregational pastor and hymn writer Isaac Watts in the eighteenth century. An unusually large number of his psalms and hymns are still sung by virtually the whole English-speaking church. Did Watts in his version of the Psalter[13] avoid justice? What did he include, not exclude? Did he omit justice? Hardly.

On the first page of his version of the Psalter, Psalm 1 goes like this: "But in the statutes of the Lord has plac'd his chief delight." And later we get this:

> Judges, who rule the world by laws
> Will ye despise the righteous cause,
>   When the injur'd poor before you stands?
> Dare ye condemn the righteous poor,
> And let rich sinners 'scape secure,
>   While gold and greatness bribe your hands?
>
> Have ye forgot, or never knew,
> That God will judge the judges too?
>   High in the Heav'ns his justice reigns;
> Yet you invade the rights of God,
> And send your bold decrees abroad,
>   To bind the conscience in your chains.
>   (Ps 58:1-2)[14]

---

[13] Watts, *Psalms of David Imitated in the Language of the New Testament*, xxi. (The book was first published in 1719, but this edition of 1768 is the one to which I have access.)

[14] Watts, *Psalms of David*, 121.

Among th' assemblies of the great,
A greater ruler takes his seat;
    The God of heav'n, as earth surveys
    Those gods on earth, and all their ways.

Why will ye then frame wicked laws?
Or why support th' unrighteous cause?
    When will ye once defend the poor,
    That sinners vex the saints no more?
                    (Ps 82:1-2)[15]

The Psalter's typical emphasis on justice, with its even stronger emphasis on God's grace and mercy is there in Watts too:

Justice and truth attend thee still,
    but mercy is thy choice;
And God, thy God, thy soul shall fill,
    with most peculiar joys.
                 (Ps 45:5)[16]

Excursus. Watts contemporized the psalms, inserted New Testament themes in his metrical versions, and modified them for the sake of length. He also left out twelve psalms. For three of these he explained why:

> The 28th psalm has scarce anything new, but what is repeated in other psalms.[17]

> The 43rd psalm is so near akin to this [42nd], that I have omitted it, only borrowing the 3rd and 4th verses to conclude this [42nd] hymn.[18]

> The 108th psalm is formed out of the 57th and 60th, therefore I have omitted it.[19]

The other nine he omitted without specific notes about them, but in his introduction Watts said this:

[15] Ibid., 166.
[16] Ibid., 94.
[17] Ibid., 60.
[18] Ibid., 91.
[19] Ibid., 227.

There are several songs of this *Royal Author* that seem improper for any person besides himself; so that I cannot believe that the *whole book of Psalms* (even in the original) was appointed for the ordinary and constant worship of the *Jewish Sanctuary or the Synagogues,* though several of them might be often sung; much less are they all proper for a *Christian Church. . . .*[20]

And in the context of his overall attempt to "accommodate" the psalms to Christian worship, he omitted some[21] and said this:

Why must I join with *David* in his legal or prophetic language, to curse my enemies, when my Saviour, in his sermons, has taught me to love and bless them? Why may not a *Christian* omit all of these passages of the Jewish psalmist, that tend to fill the word with overwhelming sorrows, despairing thoughts or bitter resentments, none of which are [*sic*] well suited to the spirit of Christianity, which is a dispensation of hope, joy, and love.[22]

Psalm 88 is one of the most devastating pieces of despair ever written. Watts omitted it. The other eight psalms that he left out (52, 54, 59, 64, 70, 79, 137, 140) fit into the imprecatory category, which he mentions in connection with Psalm 69: "But I have omitted the *dreadful imprecations on his enemies,* except what is inserted in this last *stanza,* in the way of prediction or threatening."[23]

Here we come upon a serious problem. Are the psalms themselves unjust in their imprecations? Are glee at beating the heads of enemies' babies on rocks (Ps 137:9) and asking God to let burning coals fall on evil ones and fling them into pits (Ps 140:10) related to justice? Or are these thoughts (and acts) of vengeance the antithesis of justice? Or, if they are justice, is justice of this sort the concern of

---

[20] Ibid., vii–viii.

[21] Ibid., xiv.

[22] Ibid., xviii. Watts expressed similar sentiments in the preface to *Hymns and Spiritual Songs* (London: J. H. 1709, 2d ed.,) reprinted in Bishop, *Isaac Watts,* li–lii.

[23] Ibid., 143–44. Stanza 8 to which Watts refers is this:
But God beheld; and from his throne,
Marks out the men that hate his Son;
The hand that rais'd him from the dead,
Shall pour the vengeance on their head.

God, not humanity?[24] Does humanity have any business asking for such things? If human beings do ask for such things, do they try to make themselves God or take on the enemies' evil ways of injustice? How does vengeful hatred like this fit into the plan of a God of love who goes precisely after the sinner and the lost anyway, for whom grace and mercy in Christ temper and control justice in its absolute sense? Is this aspect of the Psalter the unjust side of human life, which needs to be attacked and excised from the Psalter?

Watts is not the only one whose omissions imply questions of this sort. Watts' comments and his decision to leave out the imprecations illustrate what others have also felt.[25] This raises some tricky questions that need at least a few brief comments.

Any group, the church included, can easily become a mob. For the church to utter the imprecations Watts left out could result in acting out actual violence—which is probably at least part of what he had in mind when he said they are not proper for a Christian church. They not only express thoughts that Christians may feel they ought not to have, but they can lead to actions Christians certainly ought not to do.

However, there is such a thing as righteous rage. It can easily become unrighteous or self-righteous, but there is righteous rage against oppression, injustice, cruelty, and violence. Human beings, Christian or not, will experience both righteous and unrighteous rage. After the Oklahoma City bombing in 1995, the sense of just retribution was palpable. People whose friends or relatives have been killed in brutal ways express retributive feelings all the time. Television crews love to record them for us and play them repeatedly on the evening news. The question for Christians who live in the

---

[24] See Rom 12:19; Heb 10:30: "Vengeance is mine, I will repay, says the Lord."

[25] John Wesley found "many Psalms . . . as being highly improper for the mouths of a Christian congregation," so he left out thirty-four of them and verses from fifty-eight more. See James F. White, *Sunday Service of the Methodists in North America*, [A1] and 18. Roman Catholic bishops have discussed this topic (see idem, *Sunday Service*, 18, FN10). The Lectionary of the *Lutheran Book of Worship* leaves out some of the same psalms that Watts left out. The *LBW* leaves out 3, 13, 14, 21, 35, 37, 38, 39, 52, 55, 58, 59, 60, 64, 74, 75, 76, 77, 79, 83, 101, 106, 109, 120, 129, 137, 140, and 144. They are present in the *Lutheran Book of Worship: Minister's Desk Edition*. In practice many (most?) Christians omit psalms like this.

tradition of the Psalter is whether not expressing these inevitable thoughts is worse than expressing them. Does holding them in eventually break out into actual violence as much or more than honestly acknowledging them and giving them voice would do? Does the violence of our society act out what we have hidden from ourselves and obliterated from our worship? Has our worship become an escape from the world rather than an incarnational living of grace into it?

There are no easy answers here. This much is clear, however: the Psalter as a whole does not leave the imprecations unchecked. It expresses our righteous rage, ugliness, and cruelty quite honestly but does so in the context of our common sinfulness as a people against the backdrop of God's judgment and grace. The candor of the Psalter is certainly healthy. Much of our worship lacks such candor in spite of the fact that in Christ our rage is taken up with the most honest realism.

The Psalter also contextualizes the imprecations within laments. Maybe part of our problem is that we have lost the ability to lament, especially to lament communally, and have forgotten that our lament is in Christ.[26]

In Christ is the way Dietrich Bonhoeffer deals with the imprecatory psalms. "In so far as we are sinners and express evil thoughts in a prayer of vengeance," we dare not pray them. "But in so far as Christ is in us, the Christ who took all the vengeance of God upon himself," we as members of the body of Christ can "pray these psalms through Jesus Christ, from the heart of Jesus Christ."[27] For Bonhoeffer the secret of the Psalter is that Christ is praying there.[28]

Whether you take Bonhoeffer's position or not, to sing only one thing or one part of the whole story seems to be a fundamental problem for us. Our tendency is always to collapse the fullness of the story into its components as if one part were the entirety. Different parts of the church do this collapsing differently, but all of us in our period tend to shy away from the seamy ugliness, brutality, and hard realities that always haunt us. Could it be that individually we either avoid private confession or turn it into something superficial,

[26] See Lester Meyer, "Lack of Laments," 67–78; Ramshaw, "Place of Lament Within Praise," 317–22.

[27] Dietrich Bonhoeffer, *Life Together*, 47.

[28] Ibid., 45–46.

and then we create a society full of people on psychiatrists' couches? Could it be that corporately we privatize violence in our living rooms on television, for example, and then avoid our inmost violent thoughts until we physically act them out on others? Could it be that we bottle up our righteous anger at the cruelty and injustice all around us and then break into violence when we can't contain it any longer? Could it be that we can't or won't cry out to God with lamentation? At the very least, we have to acknowledge that the Psalter is more honest than any of that.

Precisely what this means for practice is hard to say with precision because solutions need to be worked out with pastoral care in individual situations. One has to respect Watts, who left out imprecations, and those who have fashioned Lectionaries in the same way, but we also have to acknowledge that in doing this something profound that needs expression and forgiveness has been avoided. The balance of the Psalter is needed in our worship and in our lives. For the Christian this balance always contains a Christocentric note, either seeing the Psalter with Bonhoeffer as Christ's prayer or contextualizing it by and understanding it to show forth what God has done in Christ.

A CASE STUDY

So we discover that justice is in the original prose versions of the psalms and in the metrical versions by Tate and Brady or Watts. But what if we sneaked a look into the twentieth century at a group who stands in the tradition of metrical Psalters? What if that group now has even fewer psalms than Watts included in his version of the Psalter, and what if those psalms that are left stand in a history of even further paraphrasing? Those who use the current Presbyterian Hymnal fit the description. Is justice in that hymnal, not only generally in the hymns as a whole, which we have already discovered characterizes twentieth-century hymnals, but specifically in the Psalms? Yes, indeed.

It's there immediately in the versions of Psalms 1 and 2,[29] there strongly in Psalm 72,[30] and throughout the rest of the psalms that are given as well: in "nor harm their neighbor's life" of Psalm 15,[31] in

---

[29] *PH* nos. 158, 159.
[30] *PH*, no. 204.
[31] *PH*, no. 164.

"keeping of Your law" of Psalm 19,[32] "the just who do God's will" of Psalm 24,[33] God's love for "righteousness and justice" in Psalm 33,[34] God's judgment "with equity" in Psalm 67,[35] "justice for all who are oppressed" in Psalm 103,[36] "practice your commands" of Psalm 119,[37] "who saves the oppressed and feeds the poor" of Watts and Wesley in Psalm 146,[38] etc.

PSALM 23

Not all communities who use the Presbyterian Hymnal sing all of the Psalms I have just cited, however. No community sings everything that is in its hymn or psalm book. So what if, in the practice of a given community, the whole Psalter were reduced to one metrical psalm, let's say Psalm 23, certainly one of the most used of all the psalms? Justice is there too: God "leads me in paths of righteousness," says verse 3.

It is impossible to avoid justice in the psalms. We may miss it when we sing it, or fail to live it out in our lives because societal and churchly structures or our own bent-inwardness blind us to it, but it's there. If we are awake, and over time even if we are asleep, it will break into our consciousness.

Canticles

If the psalms are full of the theme of justice, what about the New Testament canticles? They are Christocentric extensions of the psalms, which Christians have used as much as the psalms. Is justice there too? Yes, indeed.

In the *Benedictus*, Luke 1:68-79, within the context of God's mercy, we are "rescued from the hands of our enemies" so that we might serve God without fear "in holiness and righteousness." The canticle ends, "to guide our feet into the way of peace."

---

[32] *PH*, no. 167.
[33] *PH*, no. 176.
[34] *PH*, no. 185.
[35] *PH*, no. 202.
[36] *PH*, no. 222.
[37] *PH*, no. 223.
[38] *PH*, no. 253.

Mary's song, the *Magnificat*, in Luke 1:46-55 (and Hannah's song in I Sam 1:1-10, which stands behind it), is one of the most revolutionary statements of justice that can be imagined: God scatters the proud, brings down the mighty, lifts the lowly, fills the hungry, and sends the rich away empty.

The *Magnificat* is quite remarkable. As John Donne said, "it contracts the immensities."[39] Among other things, it "links social justice and individual dedication"[40] and "unites the themes of incarnation and social justice."[41] As Samuel Terrien has shown, musicians, especially J. S. Bach, have set this piece with keen insight.[42] It should not surprise us that the *Magnificat* is deeply imbedded in the church's liturgies nor that dictators find it so offensive.

The *Gloria in Excelsis*, Luke 2:14, moves directly from glorifying God in heaven to peace on earth.[43]

The *Nunc Dimittis*, Luke 2:29-32, dismisses Simeon, and all of us who sing this song, in peace as soon as he, and we, have seen salvation in Christ.

The songs of the new creation to the Lamb on the throne in Revelation, which have been sung in various versions by the church, include no more hunger (Rev 7:16), the judgment of God (Rev 11:18; 15:4; 16:17) as the just and Holy One (Rev 16:5; 19:2), and, as in the psalms, God's overwhelming mercy (Rev 21:3-4; 22:17).

It is as impossible to avoid justice in the Christocentric New Testament canticles as it is in the Psalms. Again, we may for a variety of reasons miss it or seek to avoid it. But it's there.

"Hymns" of the Mass

The Ordinary "hymns," using this term broadly here,[44] of the church's weekly Sunday service of word and sacrament—the *Kyrie Eleison, Gloria in Excelsis, Sanctus,* and *Agnus Dei,*[45]—also contain

---

[39] Terrien, *The Magnificat,* 76.

[40] Ibid., 77.

[41] Ibid., 45.

[42] Terrien, *The Magnificat,* lays this out cogently and concisely.

[43] More will be said about this canticle under "Hymns of the Mass."

[44] Structurally the *Kyrie* and *Agnus Dei* are litanies.

[45] There is a remarkable consensus among us about these, though that should not be surprising, since they constitute so much of the church's

themes about justice, both at an obvious and a less obvious level. To address God in Christ as the one who has mercy, which is what the *Kyrie* does, immediately reveals the need for mercy. That need is present because injustice—breaking of the covenant, loving self at the expense of God and the other, sin, wickedness, the whole range of enemy-related matters from the psalms—requires it. Any time the *Kyrie* has included the deacon's litany, it is almost certain to contain a petition for the peace of the whole world.[46]

We have already noted the concern for peace and good will that form the second line of the *Gloria*. In its expanded form the comments of Henderson, Quinn, and Larson are to the point:

> . . . many themes are implicit in its text: the song of the angels sung to the poor, socially marginalized shepherds who worked in a land occupied by a foreign power; the declaration of peace for God's people on earth; the proclamation of God as the sovereign One; and the imagery of Christ as the paschal lamb, which brings to our remembrance God's liberation of the people of God from slavery and death.[47]

The *Sanctus* is all about the holiness of God coming into this very world where we dwell. (The *Te Deum* strikes a similar theme, as will be noted below.) To quote Don Saliers, "As God is holy, so the worshipers are called to be holy"—which has ethical implications about doing justice.[48] The pure sounds of the violin in the midst of the impurity of a deathly Holocaust, cited at the beginning of this book,

---

historical weekly eucharistic song. See the following: *Book of Worship United Church of Christ*, 31–54; *The United Methodist Book of Worship*; the *Book of Common Worship* prepared by the Theology and Worship Unit for the Presbyterian Church (U.S.A.) and the Cumberland Presbyterian Church; *The Book of Common Prayer . . .* According to the Use of The Episcopal Church; the *Lutheran Book of Worship; Worship Third Edition: A Hymnal and Service Book for Roman Catholics.* For various musical settings of these and surrounding service texts (not including metrical settings) see *BH,* no. 666; *EH,* nos. S84-S166; *LBW,* pp. 57–114; *PH,* nos. 565–81; *RL,* nos. 564–67; *UMH,* nos. 482-85, 80, pp. 17–31; *Wor3,* nos. 251–354.

[46] See, for example, *The Orthodox Liturgy,* 32; *Service Book and Hymnal of the Lutheran Church in America,* 44; and the *Lutheran Book of Worship,* 58.

[47] Henderson and others, *Liturgy, Justice and the Reign of God,* 50.

[48] Saliers, *Worship as Theology,* 174. This is the same point Wolterstorff makes in "Why Care About Justice?" 162.

witness to this same reality from the human side, but it is most dev-astating from God's side. The context of the *Sanctus* from Isaiah 6 tells the story. In the Song of the Vineyard in Isaiah 5 injustice is de-nounced. Then, after the vision of God's holiness in the Temple, Isa-iah is called to speak the Word of the Lord: "Keep listening, but do not comprehend; keep looking, but do not understand" (Isa 6:9). "The Lord of hosts is exalted by justice" (Isa 5:16) and expects jus-tice (Isa 5:7). When there is bloodshed and a cry in place of right-eousness (Isa 5:7), God tramples the vineyard and makes it a waste (Isa 5:5-6). The holiness of God leads to the prophetic word from God, which not only expects us to do justice but smashes human in-justice and unholiness, as in the *Magnificat*.

This is not chaos. It is a reconstituting of reality with justice and shalom at the center. So it is not surprising that peace is the last peti-tion of the *Agnus Dei*. It comes after the petitions for God to take away the sin of the world and after the holiness of God in the *Sanctus*, then leads to the Communion table with both the personal, systemic, and cosmic scope of justice as part and parcel of the meal—which is to say that we are dealing here with something well beyond what is hymnic.

A whole context now needs to be considered. The hymnody of the Mass surrounds the action of word and sacrament in which God is present and active. At the weekly service we recall and celebrate the whole story of God's redeeming activity. We do it in pieces, of course (as a professor of mine said, "You can't eat everything at the same time"), Sunday by Sunday, as the church works through the church year with its various themes from the larger plot. And we receive a foretaste of the just feast to come in the broken eucharistic feast we here experience. We will have to return to these matters in chapter 4.

Greek Hymnody

Few Greek hymns beyond the *Kyrie Eleison* in the Mass have en-tered the English-speaking repertoire. However, there are some that, since the nineteenth century, have become standard in most hymnals and are loved by many congregations. Erik Routley and Eskew and McElrath survey some of these.[49] Is justice present in this group of hymns?

---

[49] Routley, *Panorama of Christian Hymnody*, 78–81; Eskew and McElrath, *Sing with Understanding*, pp. 81–85.

In one sense the answer to the question is no. Justice is not an explicit theme. These hymns are, as Eskew and McElrath say,

> characterized by objectivity . . . they were conceived liturgically [with] little opportunity for personal response. . . . The mind of the Greek hymn writer gloried in revealed truth, losing itself in sustained praise and ecstatic contemplation.[50]

In another sense, however, precisely because they are what Eskew and McElrath describe, they are imbued with the theme of justice. The *Phos Hilaron,* an evening lamplighting hymn from the fourth century or before,[51] sets the tone: the radiant light of the glory of the Father has in Christ broken into our darkness, and so with the whole world we give glory to the Father, Son, and Holy Spirit. Christ has burst the chains of sin and death, and the dark winter is gone.[52] These hymns have the sense of resurrection joy and light, which leads to jubilant song in praise of the Trinity. They are extended versions of the doxological hymnic fragments in the New Testament.[53] We bow low with fear and trembling[54] in the presence of this shining and regal glory of God in Christ,[55] and we also quite naturally pray that our hands, which have received holy things, will be strengthened for service.[56]

We are not dealing here with the psalms but with the telos of the psalms. Three things are clear. First, these hymns would not have stood alone but would have been used in worship along with the

---

[50] Eskew and McElrath, *Sing with Understanding,* 85.

[51] "O Gladsome Light," (in Robert Bridges' translation), *EH,* no. 36; *LBW,* p. 143 and no. 279; *PH,* no. 549; *RL,* no. 623; *UMH,* no. 686; *Wor3,* no. 12 and no. 679. For brief comments about this hymn with the text, see Routley, *Panorama of Christian Hymnody,* 78. For more detail and a list of English versions see Irwin, "Phos Hilaron," 7–12.

[52] "Come, Ye Faithful, Raise the Strain," Routley, *Panorama of Christian Hymnody,* 79; *EH,* no. 199 and no. 200; *LBW,* no. 132; *PH,* no. 114 and no. 115; *RL,* no. 315 and no. 316; *PH,* no. 315; *Wor3,* 456.

[53] Like Phil 2:6-12 and 4:20; Rom 11:36, 2 Cor 11:31; 1 Tim 1:17.

[54] Reminiscent of Phil 2:10.

[55] "Let All Mortal Flesh," in Routley, *Panorama of Christian Hymnody,* 79; *BH,* no. 80; *EH,* no. 324; *LBW,* no. 198; *PH,* no. 5: *RL,* no. 188; *UMH,* no. 626; *Wor3,* no. 523.

[56] "Strengthen for Service, Lord," originally in Syriac, in Routley, *Panorama of Christian Hymnody,* 79; *EH,* no. 312; *LBW,* no. 218; *RL,* no. 569.

psalms.[57] The reality of the current world order and the need for justice in it are not in any way obliterated. Second, these hymns affirmed the realized telos of the psalms by singing that in Christ the God of justice has broken into the realm of injustice with goodness, light, and mercy. It is impossible to miss the clarity of our response: we too are to act with justice. Third, these hymns are liturgical and doxological versions of the christological and trinitarian affirmations that spun out of the New Testament into the deliberations of the early church. As Gabriel Fackre says, the doctrine of the "coequal Life Together [of the Trinity] is a charter for equality in both the church and the wider society, challenging subordinationism and affirming inclusivity in human conduct."[58] This, too, is about justice. It may be subtle, though the subtlety may in fact be a strong mask to reveal the obvious. In any case, Greek hymnody is in the ways just described about the justice of God and of humanity and shapes the thought and action of the faithful baptized who sing it. Societal structures may for a time hide the explosive import of what is being sung, but the message which transcends the messengers over time— both in given lifetimes and over "centuries of wrong"[59]—breaks into their consciousness.

Latin Hymnody

The body of Latin hymnody bequeathed to English-speaking congregations is much larger than the Greek derivatives. It has some of the same spirit as the Greek, but not exactly.[60]

The Ambrosium Office hymns, like *Splendor Paternae gloriae,*[61] impart the sense of the Greek hymns. They too were used in addition to the psalms, are full of the imagery of light, grow out of a trinitarian center, and naturally voice prayers to guide our actions. At the risk of over-generalizing for a period that extends across many centuries, it nonetheless seems fair to say that Latin hymnody

---

[57] See note 2 for the quote by Pseudo-Chrysostom.

[58] Fackre, *The Christian Story,* 60.

[59] Fred Pratt Green, "When in Our Music God Is Glorified."

[60] For a summary of the Latin heritage see Routley, *Panorama of Christian Hymnody,* 55–77; Eskew and McElrath, *Sing with Understanding,* 85–97.

[61] Migne, *Patrologiae Cursus Completus,* 1411; *EH,* no. 5; *LBW,* no. 271; *PH,* no. 474; *RL,* no. 76; *UMH,* no. 679.

proceeds from this Ambrosian base, relates to the seasons of the church year, fills out the New Testament story in relation to the Old around the characteristic *Christus Victor* motif, and blends in more and more the response of our piety.[62]

It is possible to read Latin hymnody as becoming personalized to the point of avoiding broader matters of justice, as in *Dulcis Jesu Memoria*, attributed to Bernard of Clairvaux.[63] But *Ubi caritas et amor*,[64] associated with Maunday Thursday, provides balances by extending the love of Christ to the whole social order. And then there is the matter of the Judge in two of the church's best-known hymns, the *Te Deum*[65] and the *Dies Irae*.[66] The *Te Deum* stands with the early church and the psalms as a more corporate expression. The *Dies Irae* moves to the personal.

The *Te Deum* can be viewed in part as an expanded version of the *Sanctus*. The whole creation praises God the Father, cries "Holy, Holy, Holy," and links the praise equally to the Son and the Holy Spirit. Presently the story of Christ with our deliverance is recounted in the context of Christ's regal splendor. So far, as in the *Sanctus*, the holiness of God in Christ, as Saliers said, could be expected to stimulate our holiness. But then the *Te Deum* draws us up sharply and concludes,

---

[62] See Routley, *Panorama of Christian Hymnody*, 61–77.

[63] Ibid., p. 71, and *BH*, no. 225; *EH*, no. 642; *LBW*, no. 316; *PH*, no. 310; *RL*, no. 359 (composite); *UMH*, no. 175.

[64] *EH*, no. 606; *LBW*, no. 126; *UMH*, no. 549; *Wor3*, no. 598.

[65] *LBW*, p. 139; *UMH*, no. 80; *Book of Common Prayer*, pp. 52–53; *Book of Common Worship*, p. 577 (not including metrical versions).

[66] Routley, *Panorama of Christian Hymnody*, 65. Though the *Dies Irae* is not in our current hymnals, it was in *The Hymnal of the Protestant Episcopal Church in the United States of America 1940*, hereafter *EH1940*, no. 468, and its influence has been extensive. At the end of the nineteenth century John Julian, *Dictionary of Hymnology*, 1:297, suggested there were 90 translations in German and 160 in English, and said, "The hold which this Sequence has on the minds of men [*sic*] in various nations has been very great." John Newton's hymn from 1774, "Day of Judgment, Day of Wonders," is not a translation of the *Dies Irae* but bears its marks and became one of Newton's most popular hymns in Great Britain and the United States (Julian, *Dictionary of Hymnology*, I:282) and was still present in nineteenth century hymnals: for example, *Psalms and Hymns for the Use of the German Reformed Church in the United States of America*, no. 310, and *Hymns Selected and Original . . . for the Evangelical Lutheran Church*, no. 732. The *Dies Irae* itself stimulated translations

We believe that you will come to be our judge.
Come then, Lord, and help your people,
bought with the price of your own blood,
and bring us with your saints
to glory everlasting.[67]

In the context of the whole creation's song of jubilation and victory at what Christ has done, the note of judgment and therefore of justice is sounded. It cuts two ways: comfort that God in Christ has rescued us and the whole sorry mess from which we cannot escape on our own, but supplication that we too will indeed be remembered and will be able to stand upright before Christ the judge. Verses from the psalms that were added[68] explicate the sense of the judgment of God the way the psalms do, from God's governance over us to our praise to my individual rescue in that whole context: save your people, govern them, uphold them (Ps 28:9), we praise you daily (Ps 145:2), have mercy on us (Ps 123:3), we put our trust in you (Ps 56:3), let me never be put to shame (Ps 31:1).

The note of judgment in the *Dies Irae* is much stronger, more individualized, and moves away from the ballast the psalms provide. When the awful moment of death comes, the Judge demands an answer from the whole creation. Everything is recorded, judgment is sure, nothing is hidden, and nothing unavenged. All the attention now focuses on the individual who stands alone before the Judge. In William J. Irons' translation,

What shall I, frail man, be pleading?
who for me be interceding,
when the just are mercy needing?[69]

The "King of majesty tremendous" sends "free salvation," but the individual still pleads, "Fount of mercy, then befriend us."[70] Three

---

and writing about it on this side of the Atlantic in the nineteenth century, for example, Porter, "English Versions of the *Dies Irae*," 24–32; and Nevin, *Dies Irae, Nine Original Versions.*

[67] This translation is from *Praying Together: English Language Liturgical Consultation*, p. 41.

[68] See *Praying Together*, 42, 44.

[69] Routley, *Panorama of Christian Hymnody*, 65; *EH1940*, no. 468.

[70] Ibid.

stanzas later the suppliant, who moans and groans with anguish, appeals to the righteous Judge:

> Righteous Judge, for sin's pollution,
> ere that day of retribution
> grant thy gift of absolution.[71]

Here, clearly the sense of God's justice in relation to the world has been focused almost solely on the individual, and the meaning of justice has been turned inward.

As an individual meditation—which Thomas de Celano or some other thirteenth-century Franciscan wrote it as—in the context of the whole people of God under God's grace, this poem can be seen as a personal act of pious contrition. When it becomes part of the corporate liturgical language, as happened when it was joined to the Requiem Mass in the fifteenth century, its loses its ballast. The medieval motifs of Christ the judge, Mary becoming the approachable one as Christ becomes less approachable, and fear to receive Communion come to mind and fill out the context for the *Dies Irae*. The theme of justice is present in it, to be sure, but it's the justice of God against my individual sins without the breadth of the psalmist's concern that God cares and we are to care for the widow and the orphan. The peasant is left comfortless and terrorized.

The *Hora Novissima* of Bernard of Cluny (fl. ca. 1140)[72] balances this picture by presenting an evil world versus the joys of heaven, with a merciful Judge who comes to end the evil. This poem, however, is a satire on a corrupt world. It was never sung as a hymn until John Mason Neale translated the portions about "Jerusalem the golden"[73] in the nineteenth century.

The theme of justice underlies Latin, like Greek hymnody, but in the *Dies Irae* the Latin may be seen to move to a point where both grace and justice are obscured.

---

[71] Ibid.
[72] Routley, *Panorama of Christian Hymnody*, 70–71.
[73] *BH*, no. 527; *EH*, no. 624; *LBW*, no. 347; *RL*, no. 579.

3 Content: Before the Twentieth Century, II

The Sixteenth Century

Luther

What happens when we move away from the biblical psalms and canticles where justice cannot be avoided, away from Greek and Latin hymnody, to German and English hymnody from the sixteenth century on? Justice is not absent, but it doesn't jump out at you with the same force that it does in the biblical materials. The church has not omitted it in its later hymnody, but it hasn't highlighted it as much as one might have expected.

We look first at the sixteenth century and Martin Luther. Is justice present in his hymnody? Luther was multifaceted. He is viewed variously as a revolutionary, a prime mover in the revolt we call the sixteenth-century Reformation; as a conservative who believed we should not challenge the social hierarchy that exists and opposed the Peasants Revolt; as a leader who imparted a political quietism to German culture and therefore is one of the reasons Hitler's coming to power in the twentieth century was not checked; as the spiritual father of Dietrich Bonhoeffer, who participated in the plot to assassinate Hitler; and as a figure who imparted to German culture the sense of vocation that, again in the twentieth century, led to Communism's internal collapse in East Germany, allowed protests to develop at St. Thomas Church in Leipzig, and contributed to the downing of the Berlin Wall.

Anyone who expects the hymnody Luther penned to match one or more of these contradictory views will be disappointed. Luther's first and least characteristic hymn is a folk ballad that celebrates the martyrdom of two Lutheran confessors in the Netherlands and served as a model for Anabaptist martyr ballads.[1] Beyond that, joy in Christ the Victor characterizes the hymns Luther wrote, which gives them a tone similar to the early church.

Since Luther worked out from the psalms, justice would be hard to omit. He paraphrased more freely even than Watts and, also like Watts, wrote new hymns not based on the psalms. Unlike the Calvinistic Psalters, he and his followers clothed mercy with joy more than holy fear, and he did not challenge the system the way the psalms do. Justice turns out sometimes to be more implicit than explicit, but it is still present.

In his paraphrase of Psalm 12[2] the poor and needy are God's concern. The context here is the Word of God being abandoned and twisted by false and divisive teachers, so that justice takes the form of the healing and strength of the Word to the needy, whom the teachers have forgotten.

In his paraphrase of Psalm 14[3] Luther picked up the psalmist's lament that no one "works goodness," is on "the right path," or practices good, so that God takes pity on the folk and frees the "captive nation."

In Psalm 67[4] Luther does what the psalmist does: moves from songs of praise to God's judgment to walking in the right path and back to songs of praise again.

In his revision of John Huss' Communion hymn, what we are expected to do in response to what God has done for us is made explicit in the last stanza:

> Fruit of faith therein be showing
> That thou art to others loving;
> To thy neighbor thou wilt do
> As God in love hath done to you.[5]

---

[1] See Leupold, *Luther's Works, Volume 53*, 212. For a study of the hymnody of a persecuted group with affinities to the Anabaptists, though they came from the Reformed and Lutheran churches, see Durnbaugh, *German Hymnody of the Brethren, 1720–1903*. Durnbaugh, page 125, notes "the general lack of concrete expressions of social concern in Brethren hymnody" and cites two stanzas that are exceptions.

[2] Leupold, *Luther's Works, Volume 53*, 227–28.

[3] Ibid., 230–31.

[4] Ibid., 234. *LBW*, no. 335.

[5] Leupold, *Luther's Works, Volume 53*, 251.

Luther's "Gott sei gelobet" is another Communion hymn, this an adaptation of a medieval one. It makes exactly the same move. The text begins by praising God for nourishing us with Christ's Body and Blood, then ends with our going out to live in love for others.[6] Paul Speratus, not surprisingly therefore in a hymn about God's free grace, automatically includes a line about works serving the neighbor, which supplies "the proof that faith is living."[7] Or, in the next generation, Martin Schalling's "Lord, Thee I Love with All My Heart" ("Herzlich lieb") grew out of Psalms 18 and 73. J. S. Bach used it to conclude the *St. John Passion*. It quite naturally moves from "that I . . . may glorify [God's] lavish grace" immediately to "and serve and help my neighbor."[8]

In "Komm, heiliger Geist," Luther added two stanzas to what he inherited. The last stanza there is a prayer that the Holy Spirit would lead us in service in spite of trials we may face.[9]

"Nun bitten wir den heiligen Geist" was a German *Leise* (a sacred folk song with *Kyrie Eleison* attached) to which Luther added three stanzas. In the third stanza of the newly formed hymn he prays that we would love each other and live in peace.[10] The *Lutheran Book of Worship* translates it

> That with hearts united we love each other,
> Ev'ry stranger, sister, and brother.[11]

Luther also wrote metrical versions of the Lord's Prayer and the Ten Commandments. There themes of justice abound. In the Lord's Prayer we have:

> Thy kingdom come here below . . .

> Thy will be done the same, Lord God,
> On earth as in thy high abode . . .

> From strife and war, Lord, keep us free,
> From sickness and from scarcity;

---

[6] Ibid., 253–54. *LBW*, no. 215.
[7] "Salvation Unto Us Has Come" ("Es ist das Heil"), *LBW*, no. 297.
[8] *LBW*, no. 325.
[9] Leupold, *Luther's Works, Volume 53*, 267. *LBW*, no. 163.
[10] Leupold, *Luther's Works, Volume 53*, 264. *LBW*, no. 317.
[11] *LBW*, no. 318.

That we in happy peace may rest,
By care and greed all undistrest . . .

To serve make us all ready be
In honest love and unity.[12]

The two metrical settings of the Ten Commandments, one longer and one shorter, are infused with justice, as the law invariably is.[13]

The traditional Calvinist/Lutheran distinctions are probably accurate for the respective communities' songs as well as their theologies: the Calvinist communities emphasized the corporate dimensions of justice and tended to clothe God's mercy with holy fear, while the Lutheran communities emphasized the neighbor-to-neighbor dimensions of justice in the form of love and tended to clothe God's mercy with joy. The Lutheran emphasis could be construed as kindness or charity and not the more classic understanding of justice as rights in community, to which the psalms of the Calvinists point. Both emphases are present, however, and invariably lean on and imply the other.

It would take another book to explore, but one might make a convincing case that Luther's hymns are more revolutionary than his action against the peasants or his sense that the social hierarchy we inhabit is ordained by God might suggest. Exploring such a topic would require, among other things, trying to ascertain whether "each person's due" would have been helped or hindered in the sixteenth century by more-or-less revolutionary activity, whether Luther's concern about the mob was its own way of caring about justice, then trying to determine how his hymnody relates to all that. Whatever such a study would yield, my suspicion is that Luther's hymnody does not directly address this issue but is in its eschatological telos quite revolutionary. If Michael Marissen is right, J. S. Bach—one of Luther's clearest interpreters—surely got the point. Whether derived from Luther's hymnody or from some other source in Luther, Bach, according to Marissen, "put down the mighty from their thrones and exalted those of low degree" in the way he used instruments in his *Brandenberg Concertos*.[14] Marissen sees Bach following Luther as non-revolutionary but reminding his

[12] Leupold, *Luther's Works, Volume 53*, 297.
[13] Ibid., 277–81.
[14] Marissen, *Bach's Brandenberg Concertos*.

listeners that the order of this world was not of ultimate significance.[15] That and its implications, of course, could be viewed as
quite revolutionary.

In any case, despite the different emphases of Calvinists and
Lutherans, themes of justice are present in the psalmody/hymnody
of both groups, at least at their sources. As usual, these themes may
have been avoided in consciousness or practice, but they were there.

The Eighteenth Century

A Case Study

No group of Lutherans has sung only hymns of Luther, nor all
the hymns Luther wrote. If we could find the hymns a given group
of Lutherans actually sang, would justice infuse them also?

It is difficult to detail precisely what hymns Christians have sung
and how often at any given point in history. Even the twentieth century's use of service folders doesn't tell you everything you need to
know, because things often get changed on the spur of the moment
after the service folder is printed. But you can get some sense
through records we do have. For mid-to-late-eighteenth-century
German Lutherans in Pennsylvania we have the order of service
they used with its "Ordinary" hymns and the *Journals* of Henry
Melchior Muhlenberg, in which he often noted which hymns he had
sung with congregations or groups from them. His notations do not
make a complete list; Muhlenberg did not give every hymn he and
his congregations sang: he goes for pages with no mention of
hymns, then goes for pages with many hymns listed. Nor do the
number of occasions he mentions a hymn necessarily match the
number of times it would have been used. "Liebster Jesu" is one of
the hymns to be used in the service, but Muhlenberg does not mention it in his *Journals*. In spite of this lack of precision, the service we
have and what Muhlenberg gives provide some sense of what
eighteenth-century German Lutherans in Pennsylvania sang. Was
justice a part of it? Not as strongly as in Luther perhaps, but the
theme of justice was not absent either.

Here are the hymns specified in the service, a simple version of
the Word Service, sometimes with Communion as well, from

[15] Ibid., 115.

Luther's adaptations (*Formula Missae* and *Deutsche Messe*) of the Western Mass.[16]

Opening Hymns:

"Nun bitten wir den Heiligen Geist"[17]
or a stanza of
"Komm, heiliger Geist, Herre Gott"[18]

"Allein Gott in der Höh' sei Ehr"[19]
(the metrical version of the *Gloria in Excelsis* by Nikolaus Decius)

The Hymn of the Day between the Epistle and Gospel readings, selected by the pastor from the Marburg Hymnal[20] for the particular Sunday of the church year

After the Creed, before the sermon:

"Liebster, Jesu, wir sind hier"[21]
or
"Herr Jesu Christ, dich zu uns wend"[22]

Communion was less frequent than earlier Western and Lutheran practice. (It was still weekly, for example, in Leipzig at this time). When there was Communion—Christmas, Easter, Pentecost and other times—hymns would probably have been sung during the distribution.

The hymns in the above list would have been sung most frequently. The themes of justice in "Nun bitten wir" and "Komm,

---

[16] These are from the *Kirchen-Agende*, which the Pennsylvania Ministerium adopted in 1748. The easiest place to get access to this is in Halter and Schalk, *Handbook of Church Music*, 288–89. See also pages 75–80.

[17] *LBW*, no 317.

[18] *LBW*, no. 163.

[19] *EH*, no. 421; *LBW*, no. 166; *PH*, no. 133; *RL*, no. 620; *Wor3*, no. 527.

[20] Both the Lutherans and German Reformed used a variety of hymnals from Europe, most often ones from Marburg that were reprinted in this country by Christopher Saur. The first imprint of the Lutheran hymnal in this country was *Vollstaendiges Marburger Gesangbuch*.

[21] *EH*, no. 440; *LBW*, no. 248; *UMH*, no. 596; *PH*, no. 454.

[22] *LBW*, no. 253.

heiliger Geist" have already been mentioned. In Decius' version of the *Gloria in Excelsis* peace is there, feuds are ended, and thanks is given for God's rule without wavering, which has been translated "that Thy rule is just."[23] "Liebster Jesu" is a hymn of Tobias Clausnitzer (not the same as a baptismal hymn with the same first line by Benjamin Schmolck), which asks that we may hear God's Word and, in the natural Lutheran way, slips in

> All good thoughts and all good living
> Come but by your gracious giving.[24]

"Herr Jesu Christ, dich zu uns wend" is the only hymn of this group that makes no explicit mention of doing justice. It moves directly from a petition for God's presence (in hearing the Word at the point in the service where it is positioned) to singing God's praise.

Here are the hymns Muhlenberg mentions in his *Journals*, with the number of times he mention each hymn. I have restricted the list to those actually sung five times or more.[25]

"Ach, bleib mit deiner Gnade"	9
"Allein Gott in der Höh'"	6
"Auf Christenmensch, auf, auf zum Streit"	6
"Christe, du Lamm Gottes"	9
"Christus, der ist mein Leben"	5
"Jesu, deine tiefe Wunden"	5
"Jesu, der du meine Seele"	5
"Komm heiliger Geist"	16

[23] *Service Book and Hymnal of the Lutheran Church in America,* hereafter *SBH,* no. 132.

[24] *LBW,* no. 248. The German is "Gutes denken, Gutes dichten / Musst du selbst in uns verrichten."

[25] The original form of this list included all the hymns Muhlenberg mentioned and was prepared for my colleague Todd Nichol, who asked for representative hymns German Lutherans in eighteenth-century Pennsylvania would have sung. I worked through *The Journals of Henry Melchior Muhlenberg In Three Volumes* for him and culled out the hymns Muhlenberg cites there. The list given here includes only those he mentions as actually having been sung five times or more.

If one checks these hymns (excluding the ones already discussed: "Allein Gott in der Höh," "Komm heiliger Geist," "Nun bitten wir") for themes of justice, here is the result:

In the second stanza of "Ach, bleib mit deiner Gnade"[26] the goodness, kindness, wholeness, and salvation which the Redeemer brings is applied not only to the life to come but to this evil world as well.

"Christe, du Lamm Gottes"[27] and "O Lamm Gottes, unschuldig"[28] are metrical versions of the *Agnus Dei* and contain its characteristic petition for peace. The *Agnus Dei* is the usual first hymn at the distribution of Communion and was discussed above in connection with the hymns of the Mass.

"Mein Heiland nimmt die Sünder an" is about Jesus receiving sinners and leads to a song of praise because that reception includes the individual singer. In the process comes the Law, God's judgment, the gift of the gospel, and God's love and grace. Justice is the justice of God broken by God's mercy. One could draw the implication that we are to love as God loves, and given the context of other hymns we have seen which do that such an implication is probable, but it is not explicit here.

---

[26] *LBW*, no. 263.
[27] *LBW*, no. 103.
[28] *LBW*, no. 111.

In "Nun danket alle Gott"[29] once again the bounteous grace of God relates not only to the next world but to peace and guidance in the social fabric of this world.

Treating the neighbor with love is implicit throughout "O heil'ger Geist, kehr bei uns ein"[30] and made explicit at the end of stanza 3, where in characteristic Lutheran fashion praising God and serving the neighbor are joined. Stanza 7, omitted from the copies of Marburg to which I have access[31] but which may have been sung from other sources, also makes it explicit. So does stanza 8 of "O Gottes Sohn."

The rest of the hymns in this group are about other themes. Justice is not so obvious as in the hymns just discussed, though it still sneaks in. "Auf Christenmensch" calls on the Christian to fight against the wiles of evil in this world. "Christus, der ist mein Leben" expresses the comfort Christ bestows at the time of death. "Jesu, deine tiefe Wunden" has a similar theme in the last stanza, but it is a broader devotional meditation based on the work of Bernard of Clairvaux, which concerns Christ's victory and refreshment in the face of the world's temptations. "Jesu, der du meine Seele" recalls how Christ carried our sin to the cross for us, and "Nimmt von uns" begs God to remember that. "Nun lasst uns gehn und treten" was written by Paul Gerhardt during the Thirty Years' War. It is a devotional hymn of comfort that includes God's concern for the poor and needy. "Lobe den Herren"[32] is all about praise to the God whose gracious love rules over and sustains all things. "Sei lob und Ehr"[33] is similar, though here the justice and rightness of God's kingdom is explicit. "O Jesu mein Bräutigam" celebrates the joys of Jesus the Bridegroom, and "Seelen-Bräutigam" meditates on the same subject. "Nun freuet euch"[34] recounts God's rescue of humanity in Christ.

---

[29] *BH,* no. 638; *EH,* nos. 396, 387; *LMGM,* no. 208; *LBW,* nos. 533–34; *PH,* no. 555; *RL,* no. 61; *UMH,* no. 102; *Wor3,* no. 560.

[30] *LBW,* no. 459.

[31] It's given in Polack, *Handbook to the Lutheran Hymnal,* 176.

[32] *BH,* no. 14; *EH,* no. 390; *LMGM,* no. 196; *LBW,* no. 543; *PH,* no. 482; *RL,* no. 145; *UMH,* no. 139; *Wor3;* no. 547.

[33] *BH,* no. 20; *EH,* no. 408; *LBW,* no. 542; *PH,* no. 483; *RL,* no. 146; *UMH,* no. 126; *Wor3,* no. 528.

[34] *LBW,* no. 299.

German Lutherans in eighteenth-century Pennsylvania used classic Lutheran hymns with a pietistic flavoring. Justice was there as the justice of God broken by God's mercy and grace for us. As a result, their song of joy was infused with love toward the neighbor, and knowing what that love meant came through the law. There was no challenge to systemic evil, as one might expect in the psalms or a Calvinist Psalter, but the sense of justice as love in the social fabric of relationships to one's neighbors is very strong.

Wesley

Charles Wesley was a remarkable hymn writer and his brother John a remarkable editor. Wesleyan hymns have served and still serve many Christian communities made up not only of Methodists but of others as well. They are held in high regard and sung by much of the Christian church.[35] What about justice? Do Wesley's hymns include it?

One way to answer the question is to look at S. T. Kimbrough's compilation of Charles Wesley's hymns for the poor.[36] Kimbrough points out that Wesley made friends with the poor and pleaded their cause,[37] used the language of the poor and outcast,[38] made clear that the sacraments belong to the poor,[39] saw discipleship as including action on behalf of the dispossessed,[40] and wrote poems that celebrated those whose lives were models of justice.[41] Kimbrough then gives fifteen of Wesley's texts, which include thoughts like these:

> Thy mind throughout my life be shown,
>   while listening to the sufferer's cry,
> the widow's and the orphan's groan,
>   on mercy's wings I swiftly fly
> the poor and helpless to relieve,
> my life, my all for them to give.[42]

---

[35] See Dudley Smith, "Charles Wesley—A Hymnwriter for Today," 7–15.
[36] Kimbrough, *Song for the Poor.*
[37] Ibid., 3–4.
[38] Ibid., 5.
[39] Ibid., 9.
[40] Ibid., 10.
[41] Ibid., 12–14.
[42] Ibid., vi.

The problem, as Kimbrough notes, is that the church has largely neglected this part of Wesley's output.[43] Analyzing these 15 hymns, or all 7,500 (or 9,000 or whatever the enormous number is) of Charles Wesley's hymns, is not too helpful. A more instructive approach is to consider those hymns that have endured and are still in use. Ones that appear in the current *United Methodist Hymnal* provide a core for analysis. There are seventy of them there if you include "poems and responses" of Charles plus the hymns of his brother John. Of those seventy, fifty-one are Charles's hymns.

Wesleyan hymns cover the whole church year and a wide variety of themes. Though John Wesley and Methodists themselves may characterize their form of piety as "heart religion," like the Moravians who influenced them, Wesleyan hymns are not about the experience of experience. They are about what God has done in Christ and the song that springs forth. "O for a Thousand Tongues to Sing,"[44] the characteristic opening hymn of a Methodist hymnal, tells you that immediately: the grace of God in Christ sets in motion a song in which prisoners, the unclean, the poor, the deaf, the dumb, the dead, the broken, the blind, and the lame all leap for joy and sing. If you consider that the Wesleys worked in the Anglican context and add John Wesley's comment about the liturgy of the *Book of Common Prayer* being the most scriptural and rational piety in the world, the "objective" background of the Wesleyan movement is underlined even more strongly.[45] This sense was often lost when the hymns were transported to the frontier environment of the United States with no disciplined church life to provide a check on excess.[46]

Wesleyan hymns nonetheless have an overriding theme that cannot be missed. They are about coming, not going. (This is true of

[43] Ibid., 11, 14, 16.

[44] *BH*, nos. 206, 216; *EH*, no. 493; *LBW*, no. 559; *PH*, no. 466; *RL*, nos. 362, 363; *UMH*, no. 57 (the first hymn in the book).

[45] Letter of John Wesley to Coke, Asbury, and "our Brethren in NORTH AMERICA," September 10, 1784, printed with *The Sunday Service* in Bard Thompson, *Liturgies of the Western Church*. It can also be found in James F. White, "Introduction," *The Sunday Service of the Methodists in North America*, [A1].

[46] Niebuhr, "Sects and Churches," 887, perceptively describes the trajectory: "When the old evangelical piety is dissipated and there are not powerful theological and liturgical forces to preserve the Christian faith and feeling the tendency is to sink into vulgarism or into a pure moralism."

the hymns for the poor also.) The central activity that results from coming to Christ is speaking about him, not doing something like justice for him. So "Believe" and "Come"[47] and "Come, sinners to the gospel feast"[48] are characteristic, as are "tell, and publish"[49] and

> His only righteousness I show,
> his saving truth proclaim;
> 'tis all my business here below
> to cry, "Behold the Lamb!"[50]

The Christian does have something to do besides sing and tell, however.

> A charge to keep I have,
> a God to glorify,
> a never dying soul to save,
> and fit it for the sky.[51]

"To serve the present age" immediately follows this charge. That is interpreted as being armed "with jealous care" to live "in thy sight" in order to give "a strict account" to God. That is further understood to mean to "watch and pray," to rely on God, and to be assured that if the trust is betrayed "I shall forever die."

A similar turn is taken in "Forth in Thy Name, O Lord, I Go."[52] God alone is to be known in "all I think or speak or do." The singer is to labor at God's command and "offer all my works to thee" with this result:

> and run my course with even joy,
> and closely walk with thee to heaven.

Again, in "Soldiers of Christ, Arise"[53] putting on Christ's armor means standing in his might, praying, wrestling, fighting, and treading down the powers of darkness until the well-fought day is

---

[47] "O Love Divine," *UMH*, no. 287.
[48] *UMH*, no. 339.
[49] "How Can We Sinners Know," *UMH*, no. 372.
[50] "Jesus! The Name High Over All," *UMH*, no. 193.
[51] *UMH*, no. 413.
[52] *LBW*, no. 505; *RL*, no. 79; *UMH*, no. 438.
[53] *EH*, no. 548; *UMH*, no. 513.

won, the Spirit says "Come," and Christ descends and takes the conquerors home.

Justice is not the focus of human activity even when there are hints at it, as in the hymn just quoted. But justice is not absent from Wesleyan hymnody either. It is there with God, who is holy, just, full of truth and grace,[54] who heals the sick and leads the blind.[55] And it is there as our responsibility toward one another, though the social fabric is not challenged: we are to bear one another's burdens; to live in unity and charity with one another, to be one with each other as we are one in Christ; to seek peace and cease our strife; to be gentle, courteous, kind, lowly, and meek like Christ; to be free from anger and pride; to have the mind of Christ; and to look to Christ for all these gifts of living on our way to the "family above."[56] The earth is a wicked place with violence, wrong, cruelty, war, and nation arrayed against nation; our response is to have kindness "on our inward parts and chase the murderer from our hearts."[57] We pray for obedient hearts here, which seems to be how we possess the kingdom now—which we will view in glory when Christ comes to reign.[58]

The tilt changes when we get to John Wesley's alteration of Watts' metrical version of Psalm 146.[59] There the characteristic praise of God in response to God's deeds is still present, but so is the characteristic note of the psalms: God saves the oppressed, feeds the poor, helps the widow and the fatherless, and releases the prisoner.

Another way to do an analysis of the Wesleyan movement is to look at *A Collection of Hymns for the People called Methodists*, 1780.[60]

---

[54] "Jesus, Lover of My Soul," *BH*, no. 180; *EH*, no. 699; *PH*, no. 303; *UMH*, no. 479.

[55] "Jesus, Lover of My Soul" and "O for a Thousand Tongues to Sing." As Kimbrough, *Song for the Poor*, 14, notes, there is the tendency to spiritualize concepts like these.

[56] "Jesus, United by Thy Grace," *UMH*, no. 561; "Jesus, Lord, We Look to Thee," *RL*, no. 405; *UMH*, no. 562; "Blest Be the Dear Uniting Love," *UMH*, 566.

[57] "Our Earth We Now Lament to See," *UMH*, no. 449.

[58] "Come, Divine Interpreter," *UMH*, no. 594.

[59] "I'll Praise My Maker While I've Breath," *BH*, no. 35; *EH*, no. 429; *PH*, no. 253; *RL*, no. 140; *UMH*, no. 60.

[60] It is republished with copious introductory notes in Hildebrandt and others, *Works of John Wesley, Volume 7*.

There one finds less about justice than in the core of hymns I have just analyzed. Numbers 215 (Psalm 113) and 354 do include justice, but they are glaring exceptions.[61] However, *The Collection of Psalms and Hymns* Wesley prepared for public worship when he was in Georgia[62] and that served as the basis of similar collections for the rest of his life does include matters of justice, largely because of the presence of some psalms.[63]

If you look at the collection of eucharistic hymns the Wesleys published,[64] their sense of the early church's realized eschatology makes the picture considerably more complicated,[65] as the final hymn from that collection strikingly illustrates. Relying on the just social order reported at the end of the second chapter of Acts (described in overly optimistic ways), stanza 10 poses these questions:

> Where is the primeval flame,
>> Which in their faithful bosom glow'd?
> Where are the followers of the Lamb,
>> The dying witnesses for God?

Stanza 11 adds another question and answers it.

> Why is the faithful seed decreased,
>> The life of God extinct and dead?

[61] When Franz Hildebrandt, "A Little Body of Experimental and Practical Divinity," *Works of John Wesley, Volume 7*, 1–22, summarized Wesley's doctrine in the 1780 *Collection*, justice did not appear. But, as Oliver A. Brekerlegge, "John Wesley as Hymn-book Editor," *Works of John Wesley, Volume 7*, 58, points out, the *Collection* "was a book of Christian experience" in which—though Charles had written hymns about the church year and the sacraments and the cross and passion—there were no sections about these topics either. Berger, *Theology in Hymns?* 162, says that "doxology has to be accompanied by a symphony of other speech forms, all of which surface in response to the experience of God's salvific acts (most notably *martyria* and *diakonia*)."This gives to doxology "a certain priority over other human responses to God's saving acts," a point not unrelated to what I will say later.

[62] *Collection of Psalms and Hymns.*

[63] See pages 2, 9, 10, 17, 22, 59.

[64] *Hymns on the Lord's Supper . . . With a Preface concerning the Christian Sacrament and Sacrifice, extracted from Doctor Brevint* (Bristol: Farley, 1745), republished in Rattenbury, *Eucharistic Hymns of John and Charles Wesley,* with a book-length discussion of their significance.

[65] Ibid., 65.

> The daily sacrifice is ceased,
> And charity to heaven is fled.

The "Eucharistic feast," the "daily sacrifice," was gone—an accurate description of eighteenth-century Anglican worship when Communion was celebrated perhaps three times a year[66]—with these results, says the hymn: "decay . . . slackness . . . vice [where] we . . . quench the latest spark of love,"

> And those who by Thy name are named
> The sinners unbaptized out-sin.

Then comes a prayer to God that the daily sacrifice would be restored to the faithful remnant for the nations and the world. Justice is not named, but it is clear that a social order in which it is present has been lost with the loss of what John Wesley called "constant communion."[67] With that loss came another, the sundering of eschatology into realized and unrealized pieces.

Justice seems unavoidable, even here where it is not a central hymnic theme. It is not as evident in Wesleyan hymnody as in the Psalter or even in Lutheran hymnody, but it is present.

Excursus

It is beyond the scope of this study to decide whether Wesleyan hymnody at its inception could be characterized as having "layer upon layer of conflicting symbolism" about Christ as love that was "maternal, Oedipal, sexual and sado-masochistic,"[68] whether its imagery was "sexual and womb-regressive" and subordinated to blood-sacrifice,[69] whether it negated human love and finally focused on death,[70] and whether it contributed to a broader Wesleyan

---

[66] The normal Sunday practice for Anglicans was Morning Prayer, the Litany, and ante-Communion (the Word service of the Eucharist without Communion), with the full Eucharist three times a year. See James White, "Introduction," *Sunday Service of the Methodists*, [39]; Rattenbury, *Eucharistic Hymns of John and Charles Wesley*, 4.

[67] Ibid., 171–72.

[68] E. P. Thompson, *English Working Class*, 370–71.

[69] Ibid., 371.

[70] Ibid., 373.

substitution of work in the church for work in the world[71] along with the sublimation of revolutionary impulses in England at the time of the French Revolution.[72] If Wesleyan hymnody were really as perverted, ingrown, and fundamentally disobedient as much of that description implies, it and the Methodists would probably have ceased to exist long ago. Other interpretations are possible.[73]

Nonetheless, these are not idle questions. They raise serious concerns, not only for Methodists (or Moravians) to whom they are often applied but for the whole church. Here are three general reflections about such matters.

1. Hymnody, when it functions properly, embodies the deep shalom of the church with a rich vocabulary of imagery. The images it employs to express the inexpressible can be twisted, however, so that sickness takes the place of health. This danger is especially evident at points where salient images of a particular historical moment overcome the checks, balances, and ballast that the whole catholic tradition provides. The potential is pathology for a whole community.[74]

2. It is certainly true that things can be turned into idols. That sort of danger attends all traditions including "Catholic" ones, and "Protestants" are among those formed to smoke it out immediately in knee-jerk fashion. It is just as true, however, that human attempts to create or recreate a certain experience are equally idolatrous. That form of idolatry also attends all traditions, including the "evangelical" and "charismatic" ones, and often escapes the "Protestant" gaze.

For movements like Montanism in the early church, flagellants in the Middle Ages, some Anabaptists in the sixteenth century, some aspects of eighteenth-century revivals, Cane Ridge and Finney in the nineteenth century, The Vineyard and Holy Laughter among us—even church growth though it eschews the sawdust trail—the

---

[71] Ibid., 368.

[72] Ibid., 351–400.

[73] For example, Beckerlegge, "The Hymn-Book in Methodist Worship," in Hildebrandt and others, *Works of John Wesley, Volume 7*, 61–69; Rattenbury, *Eucharistic Hymns of John and Charles Wesley*, 64–68.

[74] E. P. Thompson, *English Working Class*, 369, quotes W. Hazlitt, who describes Methodists as "a collection of religious invalids." Whether this is true for Methodism or not, that it can be said at all indicates the problem, and one can certainly choose from one's own experience with religious communities (the net encompasses everyone, not only Methodists) those who seem to have crossed over into sickness.

danger is always that an experience that human beings create among themselves gets elevated to what God does.

Violent enthusiasm with "swooning, groaning, crying out, weeping, and falling into paroxysms"[75] often accompanies some of these movements.[76] Leaders like John Wesley have regularly condemned such excesses as "bringing the real work into contempt,"[77] but those who follow such leaders do not always heed their warnings. The result has often been for worshiping communities to attempt in their wake to "reproduce the emotional convulsions of conversion."[78] As Frank Senn says, experience here becomes "absolutely incontrovertible."[79] That this might be in any sense at all an idolatrous attempt to usurp the place of God is often lost on those who live in these traditions, yet it ironically forces the church back to the dilemma Montanism posed for the early church: what to do when Christians disagree about their experiences. The question of what is normative here ultimately compels the church to ask about "doctrinal standards" and "historical traditions."[80]

The issue for hymnody is that it and its music can be used as powerful though idolatrous manipulative tools to recreate the experience of conversion. Hymns become not doxological proclamations or celebrations of God's mercy with justice and all the other themes of the story woven in so much as vehicles of an agenda, in this case experience in which the experience itself becomes the content. They turn out to be about the experience of experience.[81]

3. Singing about the experience of experience can easily circumvent the responsibility of the church for the doing of justice in the world. Whenever the church is driven inward rather than outward toward the world it is called to serve, it is disobedient.[82] There are

---

[75] Ibid., 380.

[76] One of the reasons such excesses occur is because a church that prohibits physical movement like dancing sets them in motion as a reaction.

[77] E. P. Thompson, *English Working Class*, 381. Charles Wesley too "had little patience with hysterical converts." Gill, *Charles Wesley, the First Methodist*, 84.

[78] Ibid., 365. Cf. Senn, "Worship Alive" 204–6.

[79] Senn, "Worship Alive," 206.

[80] Ibid.

[81] Cf. Schalk, *God's Song in a New Land*, 22.

[82] E. P. Thompson, *English Working Class*, 368, argues that the energies of the early Methodists were "displaced from expression in personal and

legitimate differences among Christians about how the church should relate to the world, how it should deal with systemic injustice, whether revolution is better than evolution, or whether antinomian chaos is preferable to dictatorial tyranny. But unless a group takes a radical Christ Against Culture position and sets itself off from the world[83] or a Christ of Culture position that ultimately leaves one nothing to say to the world[84] (and even then), it takes some convoluted doing to argue from the biblical materials for a position that shuts out the world. One may disagree with details of his argument or his particular version of the Christ and Culture relationship, but it is hard to dismiss George Macleod's passionate logic from the middle of the twentieth century.

> I simply argue that the Cross be raised again at the centre of the market-place as well as on the steeple of the church. I am recovering the claim that Jesus was not crucified in a cathedral between two candles, but on a cross between two thieves; on the town garbage-heap; at a crossroad so cosmopolitan that they had to write his title in Hebrew and Latin and Greek (or shall we say English, in Bantu and in Afrikaans?); at the kind of place where cynics talk smut, thieves curse, and soldiers gamble. Because that is where he died. And that is what he died about. And that is where churchmen [sic] should be and what churchmanship [sic] should be about.[85]

If hymnody contributes to the disobedience of neglecting the world Christians are called to serve, it has been employed for a faulty purpose that contradicts its own being.

The Nineteenth Century

Catherine Winkworth

Catherine Winkworth was one of the finest nineteenth-century translators. Through her translations German chorales became

---

social life, and confiscated for the service of the church." He also sees in "Methodism in these years a ritualized form of psychic masturbation."

[83] Monastic groups do not necessarily fit this position because they pray for the world and do work in the world, which less athletic Christians who have their vocations in the world cannot possibly do.

[84] See Niebuhr, *Christ and Culture.*

[85] Macleod, *Only One Way Left*, 38.

available to the English-speaking world. In her period, as we will see, themes of justice were more muted, especially in white gospel hymnody and to a lesser extent in John Mason Neale's work. Winkworth's remarkable translations in *The Chorale Book for England*[86] might be expected to exhibit a similar muting. Such does not seem to be the case. In typical Lutheran fashion, lines like these recur:

> And let me do to others
> > As Thou hast done to me
> > > (48)

> Thou feedest us in pure compassion;
> > Teach us to care for others' need;
> Let each, as he is able, comfort
> > The sick and poor, the hungry feed:
> > > (181)

Other hymns, some of which we have encountered before, where there are similar themes include the following:[87]

"Against thee only have I sinn'd"	42
"Ah God, from heaven look down"	101
"Alas, dear Lord"	52
"All glory be to God on high"	1
"All praise and thanks to God most high"	2
"Heart and heart together bound"	105
"If thou but suffer God to guide thee"	134
"Let the earth now praise the Lord"	24
"Lift up your heads, ye mighty gates"	25
"Lord Jesu Christ, in Thee alone"	112
"Lord Jesu Christ, the Prince of Peace"	182
"Lord, all my heart is fix'd on Thee"	119
"Now God be with us"	170
"O Christ, Thou bright and Morning Star"	144
"O God, Thou faithful God"	115
"O Holy Spirit, enter in"	70
"Our Father, Thou in heaven above"	114
"Sink not yet, my soul, to slumber"	167

---

[86] Winkworth, *Chorale Book for England.*
[87] Numbers are from Winkworth, *Chorale Book for England.*

John Mason Neale

John Mason Neale was one of the foremost hymn writers of the nineteenth century. He represented the Cambridge wing of the Oxford movement with all its ecclesiological concerns. Though he wrote some original hymns of his own, mostly he filtered his versions of Greek and Latin hymns to the English-speaking world via his remarkable translations, doing for those repertoires what Catherine Winkworth did for the German. What about his hymns? Is justice there? It's there, though muted and modified from the fire and passion of the psalms. It's there the way it is in the Greek and Latin to some extent but modified through his nineteenth-century place in history.

To read through Neale's hymns[88] is to know a cosmic struggle in which Christ wins the battle for us poor sinners and a church through whom the benefits of this victory are mediated to us. We struggle in this life against temptation and carnal lust, always with the realization that God the just Judge will reward us or not for how we have conducted our struggle.[89] Whereas in Lutheran hymnody one prays for God's grace to inform and compel our relationships without any merit attached, in Neale there is always the sense that we can seize the grace and be rewarded for our doing.

The emphasis in Neale's hymns falls on justice as the justice of God. It stands in judgment over the individual's life, which is largely viewed as a private matter with God. Though justice here is clearly related to the cosmic struggle in the sense that God in Christ has won the battle over evil for us, implications for justice in the sense of relations between people are not drawn out very much. They are not absent, but they do not infuse the repertoire as in the psalms, and they often relate to the reward that accrues to the doer of good.

So, in "Good King Wenceslas," "ye who now will bless the poor" will find blessing.[90] But the peace of the *Gloria in Excelsis* is there;[91] we

---

[88] These were brought together by his daughter, Mary Sackville Lawson, in *Collected Hymns, Sequences, and Carols of John Mason Neale*.

[89] This is most obvious for the commemoration of the "Second and Impartial Coming of Our Lord Jesus Christ," but not only there. See Lawson, *Collected Hymns*, 252–56, 336, 366.

[90] Ibid., 288.

[91] "The Holy Children Boldly Stand," Ibid., 246.

pray for God's kingdom to come, which includes peace for the whole world and healing the deaf and the dumb;[92] since God loved the world we are to do the same;[93] and we ask that "we may never be"

> Rich to ourselves and poor to Thee;
> Forgetting, in their sore distress,
> The widow and the fatherless.[94]

There are indications that justice has revolutionary import: joy and gladness come to both "king and peasant";[95] "slaves are set free and captives ransomed";[96] things are turned upside down when in place of the nobleman, Dives, the merchant, and the rich, it's the ploughman, Lazarus, the clerk, and the poor who are invited to the banquet. Why? "Because the King of all Hath laid aside His riches, and is born in Bethlehem stall."[97] And the soldier does "strike in for justice."[98]

But this revolution is there in spite of itself. The sense of any challenge to systemic injustice or that systemic injustice might be a problem to be attacked is absent, as it is in Luther and Wesley. We are to labor, as Jesus did, for others, but to endure our sorrows and temptations, which will only be cured by death.[99] "Brief life is . . . our portion," and central to our being in this "very evil" world we are to look to the world to come.[100] The social order was conceived as a given by Neale even more than in Luther's view. One can see how Dietrich Bonhoeffer was Luther's progeny. In viewing the systemic evil of Hitler, which Luther could not have imagined,[101] he chose the plot on Hitler's life as the least evil option. It is hard to see how someone with Neale as guide could have come to such a conclusion.

Neale was generous and cared deeply about those who were in need. He gave money to the poor of the town, invited them and the

---

[92] "O Our Father, Hear Us Now," Ibid., 354.
[93] "The Saviour, When a Debt We Owed," Ibid., 335.
[94] "O Thou, Who Once Didst Bless the Ground," Ibid., 360.
[95] "Joy and Gladness," Ibid., 305.
[96] "Of Twofold Natures, Christ, the Giver," Ibid., 267.
[97] "Now Bring Us in Good Cheer," Ibid., 308.
[98] "God Bless the Brave and True," Ibid., 313.
[99] "O Happy Band of Pilgrims," Ibid., 272.
[100] "The World Is Very Evil," Ibid., 206, 203, 203–13.
[101] Luther's concern was mob rule, and that is how Bonhoeffer regarded Hitler and his thugs.

"collegians" at Sackville College to dine with him weekly, and organized the Sisters of St. Margaret to care for the sick and needy, but he was not concerned to restructure society like his contemporaries, the Christian Socialists. Doing justice for him related to a personal, not a systemic responsibility.[102] His hymns reflected this perspective, and in one of his non-hymnic poems he was more explicit.

> Well! this I say; in such a day
>   of murmurs and intrigues,
> Of Socialists and Charterists
>   and Delegates and Leagues,
> Let him who will turn Radical
>   and fling aside all rules;
> When weavers do, their very looms
>   may laugh and call them fools.
>
> What! all be head, and none be tail!
>   A pretty thing 'twould be
> If e'er our tools would take the freak
>   to do the same as we;
> Fancy the yarn-roll setting up
>   to get above the frame!
> Fancy the treadles thinking scorn
>   to work below the lame.

And so it continues until everything comes to a halt, and then Neale affirms that he'll work "night and day" before he becomes a "Radical."[103]

That having been said about Neale's whole output, more about justice enters the arena of what Christians actually sing from his pen and its edited additions than might be expected. The second line of "O Come, O Come, Emmanuel" (originally "Draw Nigh, Draw Nigh, Emmanuel,)"[104] one of Neale's best-known and most-used translations is "And ransom captive Israel."[105] That alone evokes images of justice. In the third stanza it is joined in the Presbyterian Hymnal with these words of Henry Sloane Coffin:

---

[102] I am freely quoting here from what I said in "The Hymnal Noted," 8.

[103] Neale, *Songs and Ballads for Manufacturers*, 8ff.

[104] *Lawson, Collected Hymns*, 61.

[105] *BH*, no. 76; *EH*, no. 56; *LMGM*, no. 3; *LBW*, no. 34; *RL*, no. 184; *PH*, no.9; *UMH*, no. 211; *Wor3*, 357.

Bid envy, strife, and discord cease;
Fill the whole earth with heaven's peace.[106]

Justice is again unavoidable.

White Gospel Hymnody

John Mason Neale's work represents the churchly stream of nineteenth-century hymnody. The other major nineteenth-century stream was gospel hymnody, which is related to revivalism. Is the theme of justice present there?

H. Wiley Hitchcock wrote the introduction to a reprinted collection of standard gospel hymns that was published at the end of the nineteenth century, called *Gospel Hymns Nos. 1 to 6 Complete.*[107] He said this collection "not only symbolizes the gospel-hymn movement of the late nineteenth century, but virtually embodies it between two covers."[108] He noted that Ira Sankey and Philip Bliss, two of the editors, incorporated pieces of earlier repertoires of Protestant congregational song. That is true, but they included few psalms except as take-off points, and their characteristic themes of justice were omitted.[109] Most of the collection is from nineteenth-century American writers like Fanny Crosby in New York and those who

---

[106] *BH* does the same thing, but substitutes "quarrels" for "discord." The comparable stanza (7) in *EH* and *RL* is "Bid thou our sad divisions cease / and be thyself our king of peace." In *Wor3* it is slightly different: "O bid our sad divisions cease, / And be for us our King of Peace."

[107] Ira Sankey and others, *Gospel Hymns Nos. 1 to 6 Complete.*

[108] Ibid., Hitchcock, "Introduction," also quoted in Sizer, *Gospel Hymns and Social Religion,* 5. Sizer's book is a study of *Gospel Hymns* with a breadth beyond them.

[109] William Kethe's version of Psalm 100 is no. 1; the first verses of Psalm 147 by Francis Rous are at no. 205; Henry C. Graves' paraphrase of Psalm 143 is at no. 216; Robert Grant's paraphrase of William Kethe's paraphrase of Psalm 104 is at no. 442; part of Henry Lyte's free paraphrase of Psalm 103 is at no. 468; Psalm 121 is complete in Anglican chant at no. 539; a free paraphrase of Psalm 143 is at no. 554; a closer metrical version of the first four verses of Psalm 103 is at no. 555; parts of Psalms 77, 51, 18, 42, 130, 150, and 25 are paraphrased at nos. 557–63; Watts' "Joy to the World" from Psalm 98 is at no. 606; Watts' paraphrase of the second half of Psalm 72 is at no. 624; Watts' paraphrase of Psalm 117 is at no. 672; Psalm 23 is complete at no. 678; and four verses of Psalm 40 are at no. 703.

were associated with what became the Moody Bible Institute in Chicago.[110]

Gospel hymnody pursues coming to Jesus even more strongly than Wesley did. Numbers 378, 388, and 720 begin with "Come to Jesus," and numbers 130[111]and 131[112] end that way. They reflect an emphasis that is present throughout the collection. Heaven is also emphasized on virtually every page.

The presupposition of gospel hymnody is that "The Just for the unjust has died on the tree."[113] There is no *Christus Victor* theme, as in Neale. The theory of the atonement is penal substitutionary, that Christ takes on our sins for us, and "The precious blood atones for all and bears my guilt away."[114] In this sense Jesus has done everything, and human beings are to cease their doing: "'Doing' is a deadly thing—'Doing' ends in death."[115]

There is no sacramental mediation of the grace of God via the church. The individual simply believes, is made free, and the gift of love "Is mine in fullest measure."[116] Though the hymnody itself may not *feel* like it, the imperative it explicitly gives is to trust, not to feel.

> Do no longer try to feel;
> It is *trusting*, and not *feeling*,
> That will give the Spirit's seal.[117]

One does "Drink the wine and eat the bread," but they are "sweet memorials" until the Lord comes,[118] and that is a minor note.

---

[110] See Sizer, *Gospel Hymns and Social Religion*, 7, 20–23, for a sense of the book's primary authorship and focus. The editors themselves said they included "over 125 of the most useful and popular STANDARD HYMNS AND TUNES OF THE CHURCH," ("Preface"). Sizer's isolation of the gospel hymnodic core (p. 123), which omits hymns written before 1820, interestingly enough, leaves out 124 hymns.

[111] "Why Do You Wait, Dear Brother?"

[112] "Is Jesus Able To Redeem?"

[113] "Rejoice and Be Glad," no. 19.

[114] "The Blood Has Always Precious Been," no. 208.

[115] "Nothing Either Great or Small," no. 159. See also "Not Saved Are We by Trying," no. 461.

[116] "Rejoice with Me, for Now I'm Free," no. 164.

[117] "Once Again the Gospel Message," no. 245. See also "I Believed in God's Wonderful Mercy and Grace," no. 288.

[118] "Till He Come!" no. 265.

In spite of the warning against doing, one does things and gets rewarded for them. "Small may seem the service, sure the great reward."[119] A central concern was to "choose Holiness or heaven lose."[120] If Wesley and Neale gave the impression you have to make choices and could be shut out of heaven with the wrong ones, here that impression was made explicit. One of the few references to justice comes in just such a context. Justice, the speaker in stanzas 1 and 3 of no. 128[121] and with the words of Luke 13:7, says to cut down the fruitless tree. Mercy, which could be conceived in feminine terms and identified with the Saviour,[122] in the second and fourth stanzas pleads for one more year. Stanza 5 narrates the outcome.

> Still it stands, still it stands,
> A fair, but fruitless tree!
> The Master seeking fruit thereon
> Has come—but grieved at finding none,
> Now speaks to Justice—Mercy flown—
> Cut it down, cut it down.

The same scenario is played out in no. 231[123] (and 309).[124]

> There be some who will knock at His fair palace door,
> To be answered within, "There is mercy no more."

That is followed by the chorus, "I have never known you." The scriptural reference given at the top of this hymn is Matt 7:23, not Matt 25:31-46. In the latter passage feeding the hungry, giving drink to the thirsty, taking in the stranger, clothing the naked, and visiting the sick and imprisoned are the criteria. Those activities are left out. Justice is not pursued in those directions. Justice is the justice of God against human unbelief, and it can overcome mercy. We do justice by proving God's mercy: "Do thou full justice to His tenderness, His mercy prove."[125] In gospel hymnody itself justice can overcome

---

[119] "Sitting by the Gateway of a Palace Fair," no. 389.
[120] "Choose I Must," no. 402.
[121] "Cut It Down."
[122] See no. 85, "I Stood Outside the Gate."
[123] "When the King in His Beauty Shall Come to His Throne."
[124] "Someone Will Enter the Pearly Gate."
[125] "Sometimes I Catch Sweet Glimpses of His Face," no. 397.

mercy, but that is modified by the inclusion of a text from an English Roman Catholic, Frederick Faber. It occurs twice[126] and says,

> There's a wideness in God's mercy
> Like the wideness of the sea;
> There's a kindness in his justice,
> Which is more than liberty.

Human beings are expected "to battle for the Lord,"[127] to spend their lives preaching salvation,[128] and to tell those who sit in darkness that God is love.[129] Service to the Redeemer means to "strive for souls."[130] The work we have to do is to spread the word about Jesus, not work for justice in the sense of right personal or societal relations.[131] There are two paths from which to choose, one leading to destruction and one to "joy and delight."[132] Taking the right path has to do with personal morality, being "earnest, watchful and wise," resisting temptation, standing firm, being loyal, faithful, and true.

Peace is personal,[133] allied with joy, and results from being saved from the ever-present billows.[134] (Storms, billows, rocks, waves, and water imagery are everywhere.[135]) A hymn that begins like the *Gloria in Excelsis*[136] moves not to peace on earth but to a reply of praise from heaven and earth. The prisoner is still released in Wesley's "O for a Thousand Tongues to Sing,"[137] but only four stanzas of that hymn are used. The omissions make the text more personal than Wesley's original.

Justice as right relations with others is not a concern of white gospel hymnody, though even here it cannot be completely avoided.

---

[126] "Souls of Men, Why Will Ye Scatter?" no. 336; and "There's a Wideness in God's Mercy," no. 541.

[127] "Lo, the Day of God Is Breaking," no. 69.

[128] "Eternity Dawns on My Vision Today," no. 158.

[129] "God Is Love," no. 279.

[130] "'Must I Go and Empty Handed,'" no. 174.

[131] See "Work, for Time Is Flying," no. 535; and "Hark! The Voice of Jesus Crying," no. 640.

[132] "O Brother, Life's Journey Beginning," no. 312.

[133] "I Looked to Jesus in My Sin," no. 333.

[134] "Closer, Lord, to Thee I Cling," no. 277.

[135] Examples are nos. 138, 139, 172, 415, 416, 423, 441.

[136] "Glory to God on High," no. 725.

[137] No. 731.

While it is virtually absent societally and systemically, Fanny Crosby does include "So on earth thy will be done,"[138] and when P. P. Bliss allies freedom with peace on earth, salvation breaks beyond the individual in spite of the overall context.[139] There are concerns for how we treat one another, as in "Scatter Seeds of Kindness,"[140] but they usually come from what's external to the American gospel hymnodic core: praise to and the holiness of God from the parts of the psalms that are used suggest justice; "paths of righteousness" are there in Psalm 23;[141] the people are set free in Emily Elliott's "Thou Didst Leave Thy Throne";[142] and "An' its fu'est love an' service that the Christian aye should bring" is there in William Mitchell's Scottish dialect.[143]

African American Spirituals

African American spirituals were created by a people who were torn from their homeland, had their families ripped apart, were sold like chattel, and then were forced into a state of permanent slavery. What might be considered normal human relationships were completely skewed. Injustice was the ever-present reality. The texts African Americans sang, therefore, reflect this unjust state. In the face of injustice and oppression they were created and sung under cover. So a text lived on several levels.

For example, "Steal away to Jesus" meant exactly what its poetic language says: believe in Jesus. But it also was a signal, sung as the slaves went about their work, that the "invisible church" was to gather for worship at the understood time and place.[144] Additionally it meant stealing away to Jesus to literal freedom by way of the underground railroad, or to literal freedom in some other way in this

---

[138] "Heavenly Father, We Beseech Thee," no. 189.
[139] "Come, Sing the Gospel's Joyful Sound," no. 59.
[140] "Let Us Gather Up the Sunbeams," no. 86.
[141] No. 678.
[142] No. 98.
[143] "It's a Bonnie, Bonnie, War'l," no. 258.
[144] See Costen, *African American Christian Worship*, 40–41, 45; Walker, *Somebody's Calling My Name,"* 46; Raboteau, *Slave Religion,* 246–66 (cf. pp. 296–97).

life or in the life to come. "I ain't got long to stay here" and the trumpet that sounds a few lines later[145] confirm these meanings.

The texts also functioned potently within worship services that were spiritual and political events with revolutionary import. Uprisings and insurrections were often associated with and literally followed worship services. Baptism was for slaveholders a dangerous business. Though at first employed by them for "political and economic, rather than religious, concerns,"[146] baptism caused slaves to be "sassy" because of the freedom it implied. Slave owners had to change the law so that they would not have to release slaves who were baptized.[147]

To read through African American spirituals is to know that the world is a hideous business of bondage and oppression that will break the heart of "po' little Jesus."[148] Here are some examples:

- "Lord, I never knowed the battle was so hard,"[149]
- "I've been 'buked and I've been scorned,"[150]
- "Nobody knows the trouble I've seen,"[151]
- "Mother, is master going to sell us tomorrow? . . . Mother, don't grieve after me,"[152]
- "massa's hollering . . . missus' scolding,"[153]
- "auction block" and "driver's lash,"[154]
- "This world's a wilderness of woe"[155] that "God's gonna set . . . on fire,"[156]
- sinners scream and cry "while the moon drips away in the blood."[157]

---

[145] Peters, *Lyrics of the Afro-American Spiritual* (hereafter *LAAS*) 191.

[146] Costen, *African American Christian Worship*, 28.

[147] Ibid., 57. See Raboteau, *Slave Religion*, 102–9, 226–28.

[148] "Oh, po' little Jesus," *LAAS*, 35.

[149] "Lord, I Never Knowed the Battle Was So Hard," *LAAS*, 409.

[150] "I've Been 'Buked and I've Been Scorned," *LAAS*, 17.

[151] "Nobody Knows the Trouble I See" and "Oh, Nobody Knows the Trouble I've Seen," *LAAS*, 33.

[152] "Mother, Is Master Going to Sell Us Tomorrow?" *LAAS*, 28–29.

[153] "I Want Some Valiant Soldier Here," *LAAS*, 119.

[154] "No More Auction Block for Me," *LAAS*, 135.

[155] "Has Anybody Here Seen My Jesus?" *LAAS*, 173.

[156] "God's Gonna Set This World on Fire," *LAAS*, 269.

[157] "O, the Stars in the Elements Are Falling," *LAAS*, 294. See also "sheet of blood all mingled with fire" in "Want to Go to Heaven When I Die," *LAAS*, 195.

Words like these as well as imagery of a dungeon, chains,[158] and warfare[159] all illustrate the horror of the world.

But there is an equally strong clarity that the universe finally is not made in such a hideous way. Justice, liberation, and freedom from oppression are at the core of God's being and of all being somehow, in spite of all the appearances to the contrary. The spirituals express this theme in a rich array of imagery from the biblical story, most obviously in what God has done in Jesus, which leads to baptism and freedom.

> I'm so glad done just got out of Egypt land,
> I'm so glad done fell in love with the Son of Man.
> . . . .
> My dungeon shook and the chain fell off,
> . . . .[160]

- "I'm free at last, . . . born of God and I've been baptized."[161]
- Jesus is "chief of the heavenly crew," who "set[s] a poor sinner free"[162] and "broke the Roman kingdom down";[163]
- he rules "my soul, . . . the heaven, . . . the sinner, . . . little David, . . . [and] old Goliath";[164]
- he's the lily of the valley, the white rose of Sharon, the Great Physician, my Lord, the Alpha and Omega, the Shepherd, the door, "the Rock the church is built upon," the Bread of heaven, the Truth, the Way, "the light that shines to a perfect day," the balm of Gilead by whose "stripes we are healed of all diseases."[165]
- Satan says he'll "bring my kingdom down," but "Jesus whispers in my heart, He will build it up again."[166]
- Adam and Eve "disobeyed." . . . broke the covenant,"

---

[158] For example, in "I Cannot Stay Away," *LAAS*, 130.

[159] "When This Warfare Is Ended," *LAAS*, 136.

[160] "I'm So Glad," *LAAS*, 177.

[161] "Free At Last," *LAAS*, 212; cf. "Some Seek the Lord" and "The Angel Rolled the Stone Away," *LAAS*, 156; and "Oh Swing Low, Sweet Chariot," *LAAS*, 161.

[162] "Oh, the Gift of God Is Eternal Life," *LAAS*, 61.

[163] "He Is King of Kings," *LAAS*, 220.

[164] "Who Is the Ruler, Arkangel?" *LAAS*, 53–54.

[165] "He's the Lily of the Valley," *LAAS*, 71; cf. "Why, He's the Lord of Lords," *LAAS*, 313–14.

[166] "I and Satan Had a Race," *LAAS*, 122–23.

But my good Lord done been here,
Blessed my soul and gone away.[167]

- "Massa Jesus" can turn back Pharaoh's army,[168] but God also worked through Moses to deliver the people[169] and locked the jaw of the lion when Daniel was in the lion's den.[170]
- Joshua kicked a brick out of Satan's wall.[171]
- The whole biblical story of deliverance is recounted with God "a rock in a weary land."[172]
- Satan is "chained in hell and can't come out," he's "drained in hell and can't get out" so that

I've been tried by the waters and didn't get lost,
. . . .
Been tried by the fire and didn't get burnt.[173]

- God "fought my fight at hell's dark door,"[174] and "I'm goin' to set at the welcome table."[175]

The knowledge and use of the biblical material is rich. The whole story is told, incidents from it are used, and specific passages are cited, like Matthew 3[176] and Matthew 5.[177] One senses that the slaves knew the true meaning of the Christian story of deliverance, which their oppressors had perverted for their own ends and therefore could not comprehend any longer: "You shall reap just what you sow";[178] "We all got a right to the tree of life";[179] on the gospel train

---

[167] "Adam in the Garden," *LAAS*, 66.

[168] "Gwine to Write to Massa Jesus," *LAAS*, 148.

[169] Ibid., and "When Moses and His Soldiers," *LAAS*, 70.

[170] "When Moses and His Soldiers," *LAAS*, 70; "Didn't My Lord Deliver Daniel?" *LAAS*, 162–63; and "Who Lock, Who Lock the Lion?" *LAAS*, 200.

[171] "Joshua Fought the Battle 'round Jericho's Wall," *LAAS*, 20.

[172] "My God Is a Rock in a Weary Land," *LAAS*, 85.

[173] "Hum—m, Lordy, Chained in Hell and Can't Come Out," *LAAS*, 138–39.

[174] "Rock-a My Soul in the Bosom of Abraham," *LAAS*, 406.

[175] "I'm Goin' to Climb Up Jacob's Ladder," *LAAS*, 189.

[176] The preaching of John the Baptist in "Been A-Listening All Night Long," *LAAS*, 5.

[177] The Beatitudes (and the preaching of John) in "I've Been Listening All the Night Long," *LAAS*, 23–24.

[178] "You Shall Reap Just What You Sow," *LAAS*, 303.

[179] "You Got a Right, I Got a Right," *LAAS*, 153.

The fare is cheap and all can go,
　The rich and poor are there;
No second-class on board the train,
　No difference in the fare.[180]

If religion was something that money could buy,
The rich would live and the poor would die.[181]

The psalms know of God the victorious king, who—curiously, ironically, and unlike earthly kings—is always subversively on the side of the poor and oppressed. In a parallel way the spirituals know Jesus is the true "massa," who, unlike the earthly "massa," genuinely cares for and liberates the people.[182]

The response to the horror of the moment is to flee from bondage[183] and escape it.

Before I'd be a slave
I'd be buried in my grave.[184]

One escapes it with death and sings therefore about heaven, but the freedom of heaven is not something you piously and passively wait for. Nor is it unrelated to what you do now. It's a potent presence. There's a war to be fought[185] until you lay your burden down and "study war no more."[186] God is a "man of war" who fights for you.[187] You "keep a-inchin' along"[188] without getting weary and with "your lamps trimmed and a-burning."[189] With an uncanny amount of patient perseverance you "hold out to the end"[190] and "don't get weary"

---

[180] "The Gospel Train Is Coming," *LAAS*, 171; cf. "Cryin', Aye Lord, Don't Leave Me," *LAAS*, 157–58.

[181] "Coming Down the Line," *LAAS*, 266–67, and "You Can't find a New Hidin' Place," *LAAS*, 301.

[182] "Gwine to Write to Massa Jesus," *LAAS*, 148.

[183] "Go Down, Moses," *LAAS*, 166–67.

[184] "Holy Bible," *LAAS*, 16, and "Oh Freedom," *LAAS*, 138.

[185] "I'm Going to Stay in the Battlefield," *LAAS*, 126; "When This Warfare Is Ended" and "Oh, My Little Soul's Determined," *LAAS*, 136.

[186] "Going to Lay Down My Burden," *LAAS*, 214.

[187] "Rock-a My Soul in the Bosom of Abraham," *LAAS*, 406.

[188] "Keep A-Inchin' Along," *LAAS*, 128.

[189] "Members, Don't Get Weary," *LAAS*, 58.

[190] "I'm Going to Hold Out to the End," *LAAS*, 120; cf. "O, I'm Not Weary Yet," *LAAS*, 137.

because "there's a better day a-coming."[191] Freedom could literally break in by way of the underground railroad or presumably some other way for which you work, but God's underlying freedom breaks transformatively into human life through worship and singing the songs of the faith. On Sunday resurrected life is here and now.[192]

What about justice itself? ". . . ole Satan with a black book under his arm" thinks justice means "More'n half them people am mine," but Mary and Martha know the truth of Hallelujah to the risen Lamb, and Peter has the keys of Bethlehem.[193] You have to face God's judgment by yourself and have to

> Mind my sister how you walk on the cross,
> Your foot might slip and your soul get lost.[194]

But the overwhelming sense is that with God mercy is more powerful than an absolute justice, for "God's got plenty of room."[195] In Erskine Peters words, the "just order of the universe is generative, not degenerative."[196] You can trust that God cares about the poor and needy, the widows and orphans, the motherless children, and even hypocrites and "long tongue liars" both "in this land" and under "another sun."[197] Jesus preaches to the poor,[198] and there's no second class or difference in the fare on the gospel train.[199]

Human beings are to deal with one another the way God deals with them: "treat everybody right"[200] and your neighbor like yourself,[201] forgive those who "scandalize your name,"[202] "quit telling lies, . . . and let your neighbor be,"[203] be faithful in married

---

[191] "Oh, Walk Together, Children," *LAAS*, 66–67.

[192] "By and By," *LAAS*, 164.

[193] "Oh! Mary," *LAAS*, 89.

[194] "Oh, Jerusalem!" *LAAS*, 366.

[195] "God's Got Plenty of Room," *LAAS*, 64.

[196] Peters' notes here are entitled "Lyrics of Judgment and Reckoning," *LAAS*, 263.

[197] "Lord, Help the Poor and Needy," *LAAS*, 21.

[198] "Oh, the Gift of God Is Eternal Life," *LAAS*, 61.

[199] "The Gospel Train Is Coming," *LAAS*, 171.

[200] "I'm Going to Stay in the Battlefield," *LAAS*, 126.

[201] "I Got a Hidin' Place," *LAAS*, 391–92.

[202] "Anyhow," *LAAS*, 127; "Tell, Jesus," *LAAS*, 373; "Anyhow," *LAAS*, 382.

[203] "O, Give Me Your Hand," *LAAS*, 63. Not telling lies is a recurring theme: "Reign, Oh! Reign," *LAAS*, 179; "Oh-o, Juniors," *LAAS*, 286; "You Can Run a Long Time," *LAAS*, 300; "Heaven, Sweet Heaven," *LAAS*, 409.

relationships,[204] walk in God's commandments,[205] and "live a life of service."[206] These obviously and necessarily have to do with one-to-one relationships. Challenges to the social order are implicit but under cover.

Summary

Are we twentieth-century Christians the first to sing about justice? Obviously not. In the psalms, their metrical versions, and the canticles justice leaps out at you. In the hymns of the Mass you can't avoid it. It's there strongly but subtly in Greek and Latin hymnody, though Latin hymnody eventually individualizes it and obscures it. In the hymns of Luther and his progeny you have to look a little more closely, but it's there. African American spirituals clearly include it. Wesley, Neale, and nineteenth-century gospel hymnody minimize it or may even be interpreted as removing it, and in that sense twentieth-century hymnody can be seen as a recovery. But justice has never been absent from Christian hymnody, at least not from the repertoires studied here, even in the eighteenth and nineteenth centuries. We are not the first Christians to sing about justice.

[204] "You Can Run a Long Time," *LAAS*, 300–301.
[205] "Halleluja, Halleluja," *LAAS*, 335.
[206] "Oh, You Got to Walk-a That Lonesome Valley," *LAAS*, 373–74.

4 Context

Worship

When I was in high school, my best friend was a pianist and conductor named Byrne Camp, who, after he graduated, went to Juilliard School of Music in New York. He died some years ago at a much too early age. After college he played the organ for my wedding. When he came to the town where my wife and I were being married, since he was an African American, he could not stay in the motel where white folks were welcome. That stimulated a sermon from my brother-in-law, Pastor Otis E. Young, who had presided at our wedding. In it he contrasted the justice suggested by a statue of Mary (remember her *Magnificat*) on the front lawn of the motel with the injustice of the motel's practice—a situation not unlike the justice of our song in contrast with the injustice of the way we live. My friend's experience at our wedding and reading books such as *Black Like Me*[1] began to convince me that racism with its cruel and unjust madness, if we did not solve it—and I despaired about that prospect—was the plague that would destroy our country.

Byrne and I sang together in our high school choir, I sang in a choir he organized, we argued about music and all manner of other things, and he had me listen to and criticize his playing of big Romantic piano pieces and those of J. S. Bach. In the process, on occasion when I was not conducting a choir in a hospital chapel or church, I visited his church, where he served as one of the musicians.

---

[1] John Howard Griffin, *Black Like Me*.

At the time I was just starting to visit other churches and had not yet studied musical styles, church history, or theology; had not yet tried to figure out what the poor German immigrant community I came from, which had not owned slaves, had to do with racism; had not tried to sort out evil and systemic matters of injustice like racism, sexism, and classism in American society and how I was part of them; and had not yet considered the good that systems and bureaucracies could do, as in the civil servants they provide. So I had little or no framework for processing things when I visited my friend's church.

Byrne's church was the first African American church I visited. What startled me on that first visit, and continues to stand out every time I attend worship in African American churches, was that hymns I knew had another meaning. The first-person singular "I," which in my experience seemed in-grown, self-centered, individualized, and even sentimental, in Byrne's church became a corporate "we."[2] There was the clear sense of an oppressed people under siege singing a sturdy but not sentimental song about their relationship with Jesus that nerved them for the fight for justice in the world.

This experience set me onto the reality that context could alter content. Later, it became apparent that three overlapping contexts need to be considered. One is the music that clothes the text, the second is the community that is doing the singing, and the third is Christian worship itself. Let me make brief comments about the first two and then consider the third at greater length.

1. As to *music*, one simply has to consider what happens to a text when you change the tune. What happens is very difficult, if not impossible, to define with precision. If you sing, let us say, "Love Divine, All Loves Excelling" to HYFRYDOL instead of BEECHER, you may sense a sturdiness has been introduced that serves to strengthen the meaning of God's love. Whatever happens, the words are interpreted differently. That is, music exegetes a text, and different pieces of music exegete the same text differently.

2. The *nature of the community* suggests a grid of interlocking factors that can be posed as questions. Is the community made up pri-

---

[2] Costen, *African American Christian Worship*, 96, confirms this: "The 'I' technically communicates that 'we'—'all of us'—share in the struggle." My point here is not the distinction between "I" and "we" hymns. About that I think Marshall, *Common Hymnsense*, 9 and 146, is largely correct. The point here is about the context of the singers and what that does to the text.

marily of people who have much of this world's goods or primarily of those who have little? Is it a mix of the two? What kind of mix? What about the social or class level of the community, and how is that related to the economic factors? Is the community basically one race, one ethnic group, or more than one? If more than one, which ones? Two groups? Many? How are they related? As groups, as individuals? Mostly men, mostly women, mostly children, mostly single, mostly married? Rural, urban, what part of the country? What are their histories apart and together? What is the confessional orientation of the community? Reformed, Lutheran, Roman Catholic, Methodist, Anabaptist, Episcopal, Quaker, Charismatic, a "community" church, a mix of backgrounds in a church with a clear confessional heritage and witness, a mix of backgrounds in a church with no clear confessional heritage and background? What about the confluence of all these economic, social, ethnic, and confessional issues as well as other ones that could be added? All of this will affect the song and how it is interpreted.

3. For Christians *worship* fundamentally contextualizes hymnody. Hymnody does not exist in isolation. It takes place within the context of Christian worship. Christian worship for most of the church has centered in both word and sacrament at the weekly Sunday celebration of the paschal mystery of Jesus' death and resurrection, around which the daily prayers of the church have spun. Catholics can be faulted for their tendency to omit the word, at least in a full-orbed way, and Protestants can be faulted for their tendency to omit the supper as weekly. But even when both word and supper have not happened weekly, they still have hovered over most Christian worship. Just consider the architecture of most churches where pulpit and table predominate—font too, of course, for baptism, which initiates and drenches the Christian life, though it happens only when people are to be baptized. Or consider the church's practice historically and theologically. Almost everywhere you look word and sacrament have been central concerns. Hymnody's relation to justice is contextualized, therefore, by the relationship of word and sacrament to justice. Some reflections about that are necessary.

Word and sacrament are integrally related to justice and the doing of justice.[3] Simple observations tell you this. Just after the first

[3] Parts of what follow are edited from Westermeyer, "Sharper Than Any Two-Edged Sword," 51–57. Some lengthier discussions on related topics

Rodney King verdict, with Los Angeles in flames,[4] I visited a worship service at a church in the Chicago area. A service of word and sacrament, the sermon addressed issues of racial and social justice head-on and then led directly afterwards to a forum about these matters with high-powered leaders from the city.

I have been struck by how inner-city churches that have the highest mix of races, classes, sexes, and ages—African American, Anglo-American, European American, Latino, Asian, rich, poor, men, women, young, old—and the strongest commitments to justice in their communities are often precisely the ones that have word and sacrament at the center of their common lives. And this is also striking: the pastors I know who have the strongest commitments to word and sacraments are very often exactly the same ones who have the strongest commitments to justice.

One could easily assemble examples that demonstrate just the reverse, of course. Janet Walton[5] and James White[6] are among those who have pointed this out quite honestly and helpfully. Word and sacraments can be and often are made into idols. The word can easily be turned into self-serving words or made frivolous, as Luther said in his comment about pastors preaching sermons about blue ducks.[7] Sacraments can be perverted into idols "no different from the other principalities of tradition and institution in the world,"[8]

---

include Avila, *Worship and Politics;* Balasuriya, *Eucharist and Human Liberation;* Egan, *Liturgy and Justice;* Empereur and Kiesling, *Liturgy That Does Justice;* Henderson and others, *Liturgy, Justice, and the Reign of God;* Hughes and Francis, *Living No Longer for Ourselves;* Steven Larson and others, in Lathrop, "Ethical Implications of Worship"; Searle, *Liturgy and Social Justice;* Sedgwick, *Sacramental Ethics,* especially chapter 7; Smith, *Where Two or Three Are Gathered;* Stamps, *To Do Justice and Right Upon the Earth;* James F. White, *Sacraments as God's Self Giving,* especially chapter 5; Willimon, *Service of God;* Wolterstorff, *Until Justice and Peace Embrace,* especially chapter 7.

[4] Rodney King, an African American motorist, was beaten by white policemen in 1991. The beating was videotaped by a bystander. The State Court verdict of acquittal in 1992 for the policemen set off five days of riots in Los Angeles. The following year a federal court convicted two of the officers of violating King's civil rights.

[5] Walton, *Art and Worship,* 58, for example.

[6] James White, "Worship as a Source of Injustice," 72–76.

[7] See Leupold, *Luther's Works, volume 53,* 78.

[8] Stringfellow, *Free in Obedience,* 119.

which amounts to profaning them. Or as Walter Brueggemann said, worship can be distorted "to symbolize a god (idol) who cannot act, and a social system (ideology) that cannot change or be criticized."[9]

Since we can so easily pervert them, the relation of word and sacrament to justice is fundamentally theologically normative rather than always historically demonstrable. The prophetic word of the Eucharist's word service, when we do not try to domesticate it to our own ends, drives us into the world to do justice. So does the Lord's Supper when we don't turn it into our own private picnic. The prophetic word does this in a rational, in-your-face way. The Lord's Supper does it more subtly, a matter to which we shall return later. Here suffice it to say this: if God embraces the broken creation and comes to us in the physical stuff of bread and wine, the only implication can be that we are to go and do likewise—to be agents for good in the broken creation.

"Go, the Mass is ended," then, or "Go in peace. Serve the Lord" is not some unrelated add-on to the service. These words of dismissal are the inevitable point toward which the whole service drives: "Go; be in the world what you have received, the broken body of Christ." God so loved the world. That's where we are called to be to do love and justice.

Beauty and Need

If word and sacrament intrinsically relate to justice and in fact drive it, a fundamental dilemma is immediately posed. The Eucharist is a foretaste of the feast to come.[10] It's a banquet around the throne of God. Its gift, communion with God, is the most important thing we do. That implies using nothing but the best: the best designs and the most authentic materials in our buildings; the best utensils; the most beautiful silver and pottery; the most wonderfully crafted chalices; albs and chasubles that reflect the art of the finest tailors; books that in their looks match the importance of their words.

But we are also a people in need. As Regis Duffy says, "The subtle sin is to substitute false abundance for crying need," to have

[9] Brueggemann, *Israel's Praise*, xi.
[10] Cf. James White, "Worship as a Source of Injustice," 76.

a "sinful satiety which [thinks] that it does not need God's fullness."[11] This realization or something akin to it has led some communities to reject all or large portions of art, music, and symbols of any kind.

The dilemma is how to hold together these two realities: the crafting of creation and our need, both at the most profound level. Both have to be affirmed, symbolized, and embodied. The problem is how to affirm and celebrate the fullness of the stitchmaker's art and the potter's craft along with the evidence of our emptiness. When this paradox is destroyed and either the art or its absence becomes an idol, we are in trouble.[12]

An illustration of the negative portion of this problem is the gaudy opulence of some weddings or the parallel gaudy opulence of some churches that are covered with bric-a-brac. These examples suggest false abundance that can become obscene. Contrast them with healthy weddings where the dress designer's art fits[13] the occasion and its celebration, or the church that, when you enter it, says this is not business as usual but a holy space where the craft—simple or complex—is great art yet never points to itself. It points beyond itself to the God we worship. It parallels the mystery of the Eucharist and gives our imaginations, and especially our children's imaginations, play at a deep and profound level. Gaudy opulence embraces and encourages the disparity between the rich and the poor, whereas great art used well challenges such disparity by celebrating and stewarding the gifts of the creation with justice on behalf of everyone.

No class of human beings loves beauty more than any other class; all human beings respond to great art and desire it, though there is obviously great disagreement among us about what art means and by whose standards judgments are made. But it is well to remember that an abundance of money can create ugliness as well as beauty; and trying to tear down a beautiful church in a poor part of a city has generated considerable resistance from the surrounding residents.

---

[11] Duffy, "Symbols of Abundance, Symbols of Need," 73.

[12] Diane Jacobson, in this connection, reminded me of Exod 35:30–36:1, where, she says, "art is a gift of the Spirit, the gift of wisdom and skill."

[13] For a detailed discussion of "fittingness" see Wolterstorff, *Art in Action*, 96–121.

Physical Things

Beauty raises the question of using physical things in worship. The Protestant tradition has been nervous about that. Water, bread, and wine have seldom been removed altogether except among groups like Quakers, but vestments, incense, crucifixes, and even bodily movement have had tougher going. Worship for many Protestants has been conducted in plain white buildings and reduced to words. Plain white churches, as Nicholas Wolterstorff reminds me,[14] in their essence are about the *fullness* of light, but they can easily be, and often have been, construed as emptiness. A multiplicity of words has been used to fill them.

The danger here is that the whole non-rational side of humanity has to be expressed solely in words and the poetry and music that clothe them. Words and music are then forced to bear too much weight. To deny our eyes and bodies is to collapse us into ears and minds and to force them to bear the full weight of human experience. This situation at least partly explains why hymnody and music among Protestants get so controverted;[15] they are expected to do too much.

A far healthier situation would be a balance between the aural/verbal/mental and the visual/physical. The lack of balance is one reason why the split between Protestants and Catholics is so tragic. Each affirms part of our humanity but tends to emphasize that one part at the expense of the other. Catholics focus on the physical, what can be seen and touched. They develop rich ceremonial. Protestants focus on the verbal, what can be heard. They develop rich preaching and hymnic traditions. Each perverts its own basically healthy insights without the check of the other. Catholics don't sing.[16] Protestants don't touch. To be human is to do both, and to deny one or the other is to deny part of our humanity.

[14] Personal correspondence from Nicholas Wolterstorff, September 23, 1995.

[15] That is also why, when Protestants realize they have denied the body, they often attempt to correct the situation with movements that seem forced and contrived.

[16] As Day, *Why Catholics Can't Sing*, has helpfully pointed out, though he leaves out some theological underpinnings and implies repristination, which is never possible.

What does that have to do with justice? Justice has to do with right relations. If relations in our worship are incomplete and skewed, we can be sure our relations in the world will follow suit.

Music

Relations in musical matters, which are closer to our main hymnic concern, are part of this context. Let us begin by admitting that we have accepted the culture's norm that ties music almost exclusively to emotions.[17] It's a big mistake. As Stravinsky said, if music were tied to emotions, music would be little more than a drug or dope and not worth much.[18] We've tried to use music in our worship as a drug—as a means to get a quick fix, an emotional high.

Worship and its music are tied to deep emotions, to be sure, but not in the way we normally assume. Our attempts to stimulate emotions by short-circuiting the discipline of the cross are idolatrous. Genuine emotions come after disciplined singing of the songs of the faith, week after week, that lives through the cross to resurrection and does not seek shortcuts. This means worship may be boring at times, just like life. I do not suggest we seek boredom, nor is the point that worship is generally boring; well-planned worship by leaders who respect their communities and serve them well is anything but boring. The point is this: to assume that everything in life always has to be glitzy and exciting at all times—especially our worship—is nonsense. Nothing worth anything in human life—family,

---

[17] Not all periods have made such a tie. Others periods may have erred in just the opposite direction. See Faulkner, *Wiser than Despair*, 104, 124, 173–74.

[18] Stravinsky, *Autobiography*, 163. I am aware that siding with Stravinsky here puts me in a minority in our period and raises a whole world of problems beyond the scope of this book, which can be perceived in the following literature: Hanslick, *The Beautiful in Music*; Langer, *Feeling and Form*; Langer, *Philosophy in a New Key*; Leonard B. Meyer, *Emotion and Meaning in Music*; Walton, *Art and Worship*. Whatever may be "right" here, "emotion" in this literature, and in any serious understanding that this literature represents, does not refer to the superficiality that our culture associates it with. Part of the problem is the "regressive" nature of our period, perceptively isolated by Marva Dawn quoting David Wells quoting Goethe: "[A]ges which are regressive and in process of dissolution are always subjective, whereas the trend in all progressive epochs is objective." See Dawn, *Reaching Out Without Dumbing Down*, 71.

school, study, gardening, athletic training, musical practice, the artisan's craft—is always exciting and entertaining. Anything worth doing requires discipline and some grind. If we are disciplined in our worship, then at a wedding, a funeral, a point of crisis, or some other specific moment in life—sometimes when we least expect it— the emotion will be deep and genuine because the habits are in place (and habits are at the base of this matter) that allow worship to flow. The well will be deep enough to provide genuine refreshment.

Music is not fundamentally an emotional phenomenon. It is sound ordered in time,[19] or as Roger Sessions says, music's "power is beneath the realm of emotion, in the sphere of movement itself, and the very significance of movement for us."[20] Music takes time, moves in time. Worship takes time, moves in time. Music carries our worship. It's the way our worship with its flow of beginnings and endings—in phrases and combinations of phrases and cadences—is articulated. Music is the structural substance of our worship.

Music is about relationships. It's about dissonance and consonance, tension and release, sound and silence, fast and slow, loud and quiet, single and multiple lines, harmony and polyphony.[21] All of this is held together in coherent relationships, musical relationships that take place in time. When the relationships are right, we call the result art.

As Stravinsky knew, music is fundamentally about the order, the relationship, between humanity and time.[22] You will note here a spiraling set of relationships: a relationship in music itself, a relationship of music to the actual physical time of our worship, and a relationship of music to human beings—in a heightened sense to those who worship.

Music in worship is about right relationships. Justice is about right relationships. Music in worship embodies right relationships. This means that the very doing of music in worship, and especially eucharistic worship, has relational implications that cannot be

---

[19] One could add, according to the physical acoustical realities of the overtone series, which, no matter what the musical system or style, are unavoidable.

[20] Sessions, *Questions About Music*, 44.

[21] My thanks to Robert Brusic for pushing me to add more to this list than I first intended.

[22] Stravinsky, *Autobiography*, 54.

divorced from the relations of justice and peace.[23] The relational implications of music lead to the doing of justice and peace.[24]

The relation between art and justice is not a verbal business. It has to do with the "non-discursive"[25] realities of art, with connections, surprise, realities words cannot express, emotions in a healthy—not the usual superficial—sense. Even Protestants who shut out the visual and physical cannot get around the potent subconscious realities of symbols, which inform human life. The relationships here are not normally thought out by worshipers before, during, or after their worship. They are non-rational, subconscious realities that attend our worship.

And they have a downside. If our worship and its music are shoddy and poorly prepared, our public witness for justice and peace beyond worship may be taken just as lightly. And since there are subconscious matters at work here, we will not even be aware consciously of what we are taking so lightly or omitting.

Sentimentality

Sentimentality has been lurking around the edges of this discussion. We need to address it.[26]

Erik Routley defined sentimentality as "taking a short-cut to sensation that bypasses responsibility."

> Pretentiousness, often nauseating, is a form of sentimentality generated through imitation . . . there is a fine line between pretentiousness and legitimate rhetoric. But at the other end nothing could be plainer. The great fault of insecure musicians is striving after effect, imitating an effect somebody else achieved, without the needful

[23] Augustine, *City of God,* 2.21, page 72, quotes the Roman general Scipio's comparison of harmony in music to concord in a community, which concludes, "And this cannot possibly exist without justice."

[24] Diane Jacobson's response to this paragraph is worth quoting: "like Proverbs—wisdom in creation is reflected in wisdom in art. Something cannot be true if it is not also good, just, and beautiful."

[25] Langer, *Feeling and Form,* 82. I would not tie this to feeling as Langer does and would prefer Roger Sessions' word "sensations," but the "non-discursive" aspect of art is certainly correct. See Sessions, *Questions About Music,* 103.

[26] For insights into how and why we are snared by sentimentality see Smith, *Where Two or Three Are Gathered,* 45, 48, 92, 97, 98, 184, 226.

"prayer and fasting," which can mean simply that a musician isn't technically up to what he has attempted. . . . The sentimental quality in a hymn tune is the casual use of expressive effects which in the hands of masters like Schubert and Brahms can be immensely moving by people who overlook the exquisite sense of proportion and ruthless contrapuntal integrity that Schubert and Brahms always show.[27]

Routley recalls Ralph Vaughan Williams' comment about the concern being a moral one. At issue are "failures of nerve . . . insecurity, competitiveness, and a lust for quick results."[28]

Routley's words were not popular in 1978, and they are, I suspect, less popular today. It is common among us to say that everything is just a matter of taste and therefore doing whatever you please does little harm, but it is harder to deny Routley's logic here. Sentimentality in art is sensation that bypasses responsibility. It's an attempt to create our own resurrection without the cross of Christ. It leads to bubbles of saccharine sweetness that encapsulate us from the violence of our world and from the doing of justice in the world. It grows out of "insecurity, competitiveness, and a lust for quick results."

Counter-Cultural Issues

Counter-cultural issues now become visible. While the Eucharist uses the stuff of the culture and enculturates itself, it is also counter-cultural, just like the concern for social justice it produces.

This counter-culturalness is not an excuse for being nasty or pompously and falsely prophetic. For hymnody and its music, that leads to a steady diet of what is disconnected from the memory bank of the community and grates but never sings. The gospel is not about that sort of grating. The gospel is extremely attractive. We should not minimize the attractiveness, nor fail to tell people where bread may be found as Christ commands, nor keep from celebrating and using whatever in the culture is worth celebrating and using. But we should also not minimize the reality that the gospel stands

[27] Routley, *Church Music and the Christian Faith,* 95–96.
[28] Ibid. Routley quotes Vaughan Williams and uses the word "taste," which was not Vaughan Williams' word and has connotations neither of them intended. Vaughan Williams was concerned about using sentimental tunes in worship that would not be tolerated elsewhere. See *The English Hymnal with Tunes,* ix.

against the culture and against us all in our self-centeredness. What we borrow from the culture will be subverted by the Eucharist, as Aidan Kavanagh says.[29] If that reality is reversed, the church has simply become the culture and has no reason to exist.

Subtlety

In part the relation between our worship and justice is obvious, as in the word service of the Eucharist, where the words of Amos may thunder against our disobedience. Such words are an important form of discourse to which preaching and prophetic art and music are related. In part, however, the relationship is subtle, as in the Lord's Supper itself. Our culture is not too great on subtlety, but truth is. The language of worship, of much of the psalms, of the liturgy and its music, are often subtle. They speak, as Jesus so often did, indirectly in parables.

In *Worship in the Name of Jesus* Peter Brunner discusses the plastic arts and ornamentation. He says, "The ornamentation stands humbly afar; it is not aggressive but expresses its function with a peculiar indirectness."[30] That is true because too much directness calls attention to the thing itself—to the liturgy, to music, to art, to the presider, to ourselves—and not to the center, which is God.

We should not be surprised, then, if the call to social justice does not always beat us over the head. It's there in parables, metaphor, and indirectness at the level of deep currents, where a crucial form of truth's staying power often resides. For example, water, bread, and wine do not beat us over the head. In non-verbal fashion they create a home where the cleansing bath of death and resurrection at the font propels the church into the world to get dirty on behalf of justice, and the meal at the table sustains the church and drives it back into the world over and over again.

Specificity

Just because the relation of worship to justice is subtle we should not think it's wimpy. Water, for example, can be soft, but it can also cut like a knife by slow and constant flowing.

---

[29] Kavanagh, *Elements of Rite,* 103–4.
[30] Brunner, *Worship in the Name of Jesus,* 278–79.

That leads us back to hymnody. Justice as a hymnic theme, even where it is most strong as in the psalms and African American spirituals, seems to be general and sometimes even subtle. It does not always hit you over the head and seldom if ever tells you exactly what to do, which raises an important question: if you try to make hymns too specific, do you get propaganda rather than doxological proclamation and celebration?

I'll return to this in the next chapter, but here let me explore the question briefly. Does the specificity about what to do on behalf of justice have to come in sermons? Maybe, but even there, if sermons are essentially about proclaiming God's grace, as some of us think they should be,[31] their central thrust is never a call to moral action. What we ought to do and the dilemmas of the world we face cannot be avoided and inevitably come into play when God's grace is named and published, but they are not the substance of preaching. The specificity really comes in the moral deliberations of the church at every given moment as it serves the world and seeks to discern what justice means at every time and place.

It would seem that the church's song of necessity has to transcend that specificity so that it not only includes the other elements of the message but so that it can be sung over a whole generation or even whole generations. If it is too specific it gets trapped by the moment. It loses its impact and is dropped when the issues it addressed are past. Perhaps we have to recognize this paradox, that the most radical and subversive sort of congregational song about justice is the most general. "General" here does not mean "abstract," that which stands apart from concrete realities. It means what is not limited to one time, place, person, or group.

To apply this to our present moment suggests that we can sing together and affirm that under the reign of Christ we must live justly, but we can disagree and will deliberate about what that means specifically for action concerning war and peace, how a nation should order its priorities and conduct its life within and beyond its borders, abortion, homosexuality, classism, racism, sexism, and every other moral dilemma we confront.

---

[31] That includes both some of us who stand in a Pauline Reformation stream and Roman Catholics like Hilkert, *Naming Grace: Preaching and the Sacramental Imagination.*

Under normal circumstances everything said in the last paragraph is true. There are abnormal circumstances, however, when some actions are so hideous as to become untenable and heretical. Apartheid, slavery, and killing Jews are examples from our history. It may be that only a small portion of the church has the courage to be faithful in the face of evils like these, and at such times that small portion is regretfully compelled to stand alone. Even then, perhaps especially then, I suspect Mary's song or one like it that remembers into the future under God in Christ, remains more potent than a newly composed hymn that attacks the specific evil in question. The specific attack that grows out of Mary's song has to come in words and deeds elsewhere.

5 Hymnody and Justice

Our hymnody and the worship in which it is located, with its music and visual art, can be perverted. Hymnody and its context can all be an empty shell, ingrown, self-centered, and even evil. Such a perversion is the ever-present danger. We dare not forget Amos' "Thus says the Lord: I hate your assemblies, take away the noise of your songs, I will not listen to the melody of your harps, but let justice roll down." There are times when such words need to be uttered, which is why the worshiping community against whom they are directed has itself preserved them.

But as we noted earlier, Amos was attacking the perversion, not the thing itself. The problem lies not with hymnody but with our self-serving misuse of it. Amos' words themselves are poetic and musical. The cadences of all prophetic utterances are poetic and musical. Poetry and music carry the attack on their own perversion.

As also noted earlier, Protestants are among those who are formed to smoke out the perversion. They are always wary about being too cozy and ingrown in their worship. That's how they're programmed, to attack at the slightest hint of habit. And that leads to the biggest Protestant danger, especially in the American context: to attack even when there is nothing left to attack but the last attack. The downside of the marvelous lively American experiment[1] is the tradition of attacking tradition, even when there's virtually nothing left of the tradition to attack.

---

[1] The phrase here is from Mead, *The Lively Experiment*.

What happens, then, is a continual attempt to try to be more and more relevant. We spend all our time trying to get rid of the old no matter how new it may be. We figure out how to be new[2] over and over again, trying to think up new structures and forms. In the process we forget to feed the poor, care for the hungry, or attack sexism, racism, classism, homophobia, and systemic injustice generally. The peculiar Protestant temptation is to become ingrown precisely in attempting not to be ingrown. That may well be why the most potent cries for justice often come from the most ancient liturgical and musical traditions. Though those traditions can become as isolated and ingrown as any other ones, people who live in them do not have to contend so much with the futility of attempting to devise new "relevant" structures and forms that invariably over time revert to the old ones anyway; they can get the message straight and spend more of their time on behalf of the world we are all called to serve.

Violence and Being Silenced

The world we are called to serve is a violent one. Whether we have all been actually used, misused, violated, raped or not, we all see images of human abuse all around us—in the commercial culture of advertising, on television, at the movies, in musical groups and their recordings, in art, in the news. Whether this is good or bad (the abuse obviously is bad; whether seeing it, or how much seeing it, is good or bad is the dilemma) raises the question of how free and responsible speech relate, the whole series of issues connected with Watts leaving out imprecations, and how we use or respond to all this.

I do not intend to engage further in that debate, which is beyond the scope of this study. I do want to say this, however. Rape victims

---

[2] This involves a superficial use of the word "new," not what the Bible means by "new," as in "new song." The issue for the biblical mentality is not a literally new song, which would mean nothing could be sung more than once since the second time is already old, but a song infused with the new life God offers—life that is not the old all over again but qualitatively new life incarnated in the stuff of this creation in which we live, "a foretaste of the feast to come." Repetition, then, is not only possible but a welcome necessity for created, habitual beings.

96

often are physically silenced: they literally can't sing. And the society as a whole that witnesses this violence all around it is metaphorically and then eventually physically silenced as well.

As a society we tend not to sing. There are feeble attempts to sing among us, to be sure. They happen when we sing "Happy Birthday" at birthday parties or the national anthem by a few people at sporting events. Some concerts include singing, usually ones where the audience is a select group that knows the music of the performers. The most potent singing over the longest time comes from congregations of worshipers where misguided or incompetent leadership has not stifled the song.

The reasons for our not singing as a people cover a wide range: being told or made to feel that we could not sing, usually at a pivotal age by a respected music teacher or parental figure; shame in a society that feels any natural human song must not be done, that only professionals sing; a sexist sense that singing is only domestic and feminine;[3] a self-consciousness that resists singing versus a world-consciousness that sings instinctively;[4] and an Anglo-American mind-set that, as Alan Luff says, fits into the sort of culture in which you are assumed to be amusical unless you prove otherwise and to monotonic models of this presupposition in childhood.[5] To these reasons, the violence of the society has to be added. It silences us.

Song, Justice, and Health

Hymn singing breaks the tyranny of this silence. It relates to the elemental human drive to sing.[6] In worship it relates to an even more potent drive because it is about God's grace and our response. It is about health and shalom, with the deepest sort of human peace and healing. That is, hymn singing is not an esoteric activity. It is

---

[3] This may be partly a legacy from Moody and Sankey. See Sizer, *Gospel Hymns and Social Religion*, 23, 83–110.

[4] See Faulkner, *Wiser Than Despair*, 205.

[5] Alan Luff, former precentor at Westminster Abbey, says there are two kinds of cultures, those that assume you are musical unless you prove otherwise, and those that assume you are amusical unless you prove otherwise. Historic Welsh and German culture fit the first model, Anglo-American culture the second.

[6] See Westermeyer, "To Be Human Is to Sing," 4–8.

tied to God's incredible gift of sound and to the social fabric at a deep level. A just society is a healthy society. It will sing. Healthy individuals will sing, not only alone, but with one another. A faithful church will teach itself and its society to sing so that individuals use their voices in a healthy way and blend them in communal song, a form of mournful and celebrative shalom that is always greater than the sum of its individual parts.

Healthy singing happens in a healthy church, but behind that lies the necessity of making musical choices. Someone has to decide what a community will sing. What, then, about the relation of justice to choice of hymnody and music to go with it, or to choice of church music in general? This matter regularly sets the church at war.

C. S. Lewis perceptively analyzes this problem. He says what we do in church should glorify God or edify the people or both, and that edifying is always glorifying but glorifying is not always edifying because what edifies one may not edify another.[7] A blessing rests on those who genuinely sacrifice their own desires on behalf of the other, but what generally happens is the "opposite situation"

> where the musician is filled with the pride of skill or the virus of emulation and looks with contempt on the unappreciative congregation, or where the unmusical, complacently entrenched in their own ignorance and conservatism, look with the restless and resentful hostility of an inferiority complex on all who would try to improve their taste—there, we may be sure, all that both offer is unblessed and the spirit that moves in them is not the Holy Ghost.[8]

The result of this wickedness is that music becomes the gang songs of the church, in which groups and individuals take up cudgels against one another with manipulative tactics, power plays, brute force, hostility, and rampant injustice. As C. S. Lewis says so well, "The problem is never a merely musical one."[9] It is ethical. It has to do with how we treat one another. It has to do with love and justice.

Though C. S. Lewis' analysis is very helpful, the way he runs out his logic ultimately leads to avoiding music altogether. The defect in such logic is that it leads to avoiding everything. Unless you want the contradiction of a non-incarnational gospel in which there is a radical

---

[7] Lewis, *Christian Reflections*, 94–99.
[8] Ibid., 97.
[9] Ibid.

split between flesh and spirit[10] or a community from which God's gift of communal sound is absent, this solution won't work. The Christian gospel is about grace and a community that, however imperfectly, enfleshes a way of doing things that is different from the world's way. It uses music and everything else, therefore, knowing that the whole good but fallen creation is cracked and sin-soaked but knowing two more fundamental realities: (1) that God—in, with, and under the bread and wine on the Communion table—uses the physical things of the creation in all their broken condition and (2) that we can disagree and live together because our life together is dependent on God and God's grace, not our agreements or disagreements.

There are no easy solutions. We still have to figure out what we will choose. That is no simple matter, but we can be clear about some things.

1. Sentimentality with its competitiveness and lust for quick results is not the private property of any group. Those who argue for the "classical" and those who argue for the "popular" get equally sentimental, especially at points of their own nostalgia. Those points are often associated with repristinations of a past, either far or near in time, that actually never existed and generate games of make-believe. They are also tied to music that is related to certain events and emotions that one tries to replicate, as Routley says, by short-circuiting the necessary discipline.

2. Nor is snobbery one group's private preserve. Snobbery is usually associated with the "high art" partisans, and they need to confess their sins. They often have been obnoxious in the contempt they have shown for those who do not come from their own elite tribe. But "popular" partisans have often acted the same way. Dorothy Sayer's phrase, "the snobbery of the banal," is an apt one.[11] In recent years it seems that those who espouse the snobbery of the banal have become more vicious and tribal than their opposites.

3. The high-art versus folk-art or classical versus popular distinctions that are often used in discussions like this are faulty. Not everything ought to be used, but the issue is not what is "high" or "low." It's what is well crafted and broken to the gospel, in whatever idiom or style—the best "folk" art and the best "high" art—on

---

[10] As in Ulrich Zwingli, for whom such a distinction led to abandoning all hymnody and music. See Charles Garside, Jr., *Zwingli and the Arts.*

[11] See Gaeberlein, *The Christian, the Arts, and Truth,* 51.

behalf of the people who will sing and hear it. There are texts and music that express the Christian story, and there are texts and music that do not. There are texts and music that are crafted well enough to be worth people's time and effort, and there are those that are not. The Christian community will sort this out over time, keeping what is worthwhile and discarding what is not. The church musician's task is to sort it out as soon as possible, with just, loving care and all the mistakes human beings inevitably make, so that communities don't waste their time on what will ultimately serve them poorly.

We have come upon an important matter. In spite of all the cheap talk about throwaway texts and music, the norm is not throwaway. There obviously are and should be throwaway hymns, but they cannot be the norm. What the church sings needs to last over long periods of time so that it can serve generations. It is for old people and young people and those in between. It has to provide a song for people of all ages to sing together, a song people can grow into, not out of. People need to be able to remember their story, to mark births, deaths, and all the other significant events of their lives in a communal song that endures over time and is not torn apart by normal human divisions but is united in Christ. The unity in Christ of this life is always broken musically and in other ways, but avoiding it as if it were unimportant is itself unjust.

The real problem, however, is that the church's internal disputes siphon off time, thought, energy, and resources so that the world is neglected. The real problem is that the church that battles wickedly with itself omits battling injustice and doing justice in the world. It engages in our generation's version of how many angels can dance on the head of a pin.

Does Justice Sing?

In the Christian scheme of things justice is always tempered by mercy and forgiveness. As Will D. Campbell said when asked to express the Christian message in ten words or less, "We're all bastards but God loves us anyway."[12] Human history indicates that we always fail to live the way of God's gift of justice, of moral rightness and blessed relational living, which the Decalogue provides. The

---

[12] Campbell, *Brother to a Dragonfly*, 220.

cross of Christ indicates that God rescues us from our perverted in-grown and immoral unrighteousness anyway.

Our activity in this world both as individuals and nations is called, like God's, to be tempered by mercy and forgiveness.[13] As God has mercy and forgives, so we are to have mercy and forgive. The final Christian word is not some sort of absolute justice that turns into revenge. The final word is grace.

Christians have viewed this economy in different ways. Not only has the emphasis been placed more or less on the individual or the societal sides of human responsibilities but the character of human doing has been regarded differently. To sing Wesley's hymns is to assume you can get on the right track and grow in grace toward holy living. To sing Neale's hymns suggests you can lay hold of the victory God has won in Christ, and your works count for something in this process. To sing Luther's hymns is to celebrate God's grace and to pray for grace to live for the neighbor, but works are not merit in any sense.[14]

These are important confessional matters. We in our day tend to take them lightly, but they invariably pop up when a church starts to talk about anything in human life that moves beyond the superficial. Though I throw in my lot with the Lutheran perspec-tive, my point here is not to debate that. The point here is that in classic Christian hymnody justice is part of a richly layered texture in which grace, mercy, and forgiveness—however they are con-ceived—are critical components.

Justice therefore almost always crops up in Christian hymnody, not only in the psalms but even where it is not such a central fea-ture. That raises the question we began with, does justice sing? More precisely, is it possible for justice not to be a theme of Chris-tian hymnody? Can we not sing it?

Matters between God and human beings and between human beings themselves like moral rightness, equity, right relations, righteousness, and peace—in the context of God's grace, mercy, and forgiveness—are impossible to avoid in the Christian scheme

---

[13] Shriver, *An Ethic for Enemies*, makes the radical proposal that forgive-ness is not just for personal ethics but for the political process.

[14] Francis Williamson, in a book he is readying for publication called *Ears to Hear . . . Tongues to Sing: Church Music as Pastoral Theology*, sees paradigms behind these approaches based on Niebuhr's types in *Christ and Culture*.

of things. It is hard to see then how they would not be part of Christian hymn singing. It is no accident that they have been part of Christian hymn singing.

The Whole

We are led back to a question raised in the last chapter, whether it is possible to sing about any of these things without the other ones or with one thing or some things emphasized at the expense of the other ones. Of course such singing *is* theoretically possible, but the deeper issue is this. If an individual or a community practices pushing its agenda over against the whole story and the experience of the whole church catholic, is the result power plays and propaganda rather than doxology, proclamation, and celebration?

Two issues are involved. The first is that two realities about hymn singing need to be held in tension. One is that Christian communities have to sing what they know in an idiom they know. That has been sadly neglected and even attacked among us. It needs to be affirmed, strongly. Without what people know they cease to be. If you take away a people's memory, you take away their being, just as Alzheimer's takes away an individual's being.

But another equally strong affirmation has to be made. Given the propensity of human beings to turn their memory inward and to become ingrown and self-serving, it behooves Christians to sing their whole story. That includes a wide variety of hymns and music that stretches their parochial selves into the catholic whole and its self-critical essence. The Christian story is richly layered with themes the church year and Lectionary continually help to remind us of. It is also richly layered in its texts and music from around the world in the past and the present. Trying to collapse it into one favorite thing or one musical or textual repertoire is an ever-present temptation, a sectarian rut from which the catholicity of the whole church helps to rescue us. Said another way, if you sing the fullness of the story, it turns out to be prophetic. If you collapse it into the themes of your one fragmentary moment, it evaporates, or, as Robert Brusic says, "achieves a heretical density."

So the first issue here is the healthy tension that has to be maintained between a certain parochial time and place on the one hand and the broader catholic ballast that extends beyond a given time and place on the other.

The second issue is more oriented to the content of justice, with which we began. Walter Rauschenbusch, one of the leaders of the "social gospel" at the beginning of the twentieth century, translated gospel hymns into German, added other translations, and with Ira Sankey edited them into a collection called *Evangeliums Lieder*.[15] He then had second thoughts, not only about gospel hymnody but about Christian hymnody more generally. He decided that hymns were basically about "private redemption," not "social redemption."[16] They yearn for the world to come, he thought, but don't express concern for life here and now.[17]

> . . . they call us from personal sins to a personal cross; they persuade us to give to and serve Christ, without, however, connecting such service to our fellowmen. Many songs have a partial message of service, but this service is too often for personal gains of bliss or heavenly reward, or in order to secure special blessing.[18]

Rauschenbusch argued that "we need . . . social expressions of emotion and purpose. If [we] cannot find them, [we] must create them."[19]

Jon Michael Spencer, who has chronicled Rauschenbusch's position, has taken a similar one for the African American heritage. He traces the history of black hymnody, then argues that the reality is implicit in the hymnological

> history: the black church still tends to be held captive by a kind of theological, doctrinal, and social backwardness that works to stifle impetus toward black self-identity and self-determination in the larger social milieu.[20]

Spencer's solution goes like this:

> By what means, then, can Afro-Christians more rapidly alleviate these problems that are reflected in black church hymnody and progress,

---

[15] Rauschenbusch and Sankey, *Evangeliums-Lieder*.

[16] See Spencer, "Hymns of the Social Awakening," 18.

[17] Ibid.

[18] Ibid.

[19] Ibid. There were a couple of attempts at this early in the twentieth century: Coffin and Vernon, *Hymns for the Kingdom of God*; Mussey, *Social Hymns of Brotherhood and Aspiration*.

[20] Spencer, *Black Hymnody*, 200.

via the vehicle of their religion, toward racial liberation? First of all, it must be recognized that the problem is not simply *reflected* in the hymnody; to a considerable degree the problem *is* the hymnody. Replacing extant hymnody with a radically aggressive song that realistically remembers past obstacles African Americans have overcome certainly would help launch the race toward the achievement of corporate personhood. Such a new corpus of church music could build upon the base of the spirituals and Civil Rights songs to include modern expressions of faith and worship that cross the moods and meanings of antislavery and Social Gospel hymnody.[21]

Several things need to be said about the position that Rauschenbusch, Spencer, and others like them have taken. First, is the analysis correct? In part the answer is yes. One can find sectors of the church's hymns—Charles Wesley's, John Mason Neale's, and gospel hymnody, for example—that can be perceived as more oriented toward the individual and individual redemption than toward the social order or responsibilities of justice to the neighbor.

Even with these examples, however, things are not so neat. Methodists who have sung Wesley's hymns have in fact been, as Richard Drake suggested to me at the Montreat lectures in 1995, one of the great social-action churches, even if much of their hymnody doesn't seem to suggest that.[22] The Wesleys tied personal and social holiness together, which explains why Methodists established schools for coal miners' children, worked for medical care for the poor, and opposed the slave trade and cruel treatment of prisoners.[23] Erik Routley, speaking of the Wesleyan context, says,

> It has been shown over and over again by historians that if you name a movement of social reform—the education of the poor, the improvement of prisons, the change of attitude towards the sick and the mentally handicapped, the abolition of slavery, there is an evangelical behind it.[24]

---

[21] Ibid., 200–201. Spencer has worked this out more fully in *Sing a New Song*.

[22] For a study about Wesleyan worship and care for the poor see Tucker, "Liturgical Expressions of Care for the Poor in the Wesleyan Tradition," 51–64.

[23] Young, *Music of the Heart*, 164.

[24] Routley, *Short History of English Church Music*, 43–44. There is nothing surprising here when you consider that already as part of their "Holy Club"

When you move to John Mason Neale's hymns, their cosmic *Christus Victor* motif implies a concern for the social order that they may not seem explicitly to suggest, and Episcopalians like William Stringfellow have made the connections.[25] So did the Oxford Movement in its concern for the poor and working class. Neale fits into the Cambridge-Camden portion of this movement, and Francis Williamson wants to suggest that he can be viewed broadly in the context of the Oxford Movement's concern that church authority was being turned over to a Parliament with little confessional interest and is therefore connected in some sense with F. D. Maurice and by implication with social concerns. Those who have sung gospel hymns have clothed and fed the homeless at missions and spawned benevolent societies,[26] though their hymnody may not appear to have included such a motif very strongly. This could be seen as kindness within a system of injustice, but there are those who, through just such activity, have been impelled to challenge the system.

The analysis is more correct in that the church has sung things antithetical to its message, and it has dragged its feet in making corrections when these things became evident. Spencer is correct about the social Darwinism of "From Greenland's Icy Mountains"; Brian Wren is correct that hymnic language has often been overwhelmingly androcentric and patriarchal,[27] hymnody has been used to keep the poor in their place,[28] and the church has often resisted even discussing these matters. One could surely make a case in our day that many churches are more concerned in their hymnody to massage

---

at Oxford University in 1729 ff., John and Charles Wesley's "methods" included both a sacramental recovery and a concern for the sick and imprisoned. See Gill, *Charles Wesley, the First Methodist*, 41.

[25] See Stringfellow, *Free in Obedience*; idem, *My People Is the Enemy*; idem, *Private and Public Faith*.

[26] See Sizer, *Gospel Hymns and Social Religion*, 72–73. The societies emphasized individual morality but also moved to systemic societal matters like slavery.

[27] See Wren, *What Language Shall I Borrow?*

[28] "All Things Bright and Beautiful," for example, has this stanza, though few hymnals in our period have included it:

The rich man in his castle,
The poor man at his gate,
God made them, high or lowly,
And order'd their estate.

their own feelings than to sing the broader story of justice, mercy, and all the rest of it.

In part, however, the analysis is not correct. If the psalmodic underlay of Christian hymnody is taken into account, the metrical Psalters it has spawned, the canticles, the hymns of the Mass, classic Greek and Latin hymnody, Lutheran hymnody, and African American spirituals, the analysis is wrong. In all these repertoires justice is part and parcel of the package, not alone, to be sure, but a central part of the whole story of God's merciful doing and our faltering response in poetic and musical form, which is prayed, proclaimed, and celebrated.

That leads back to a question not unlike the one raised earlier. If in your hymnody you separate justice out of the mix and apply it with your own precise twist to the moment, do you lose it as well as the rest? Do you get propaganda, not Christian doxology, proclamation, and celebration? For example, here is a Chartist hymn from the nineteenth century:

> See the brave, ye spirit-broken,
>   Who uphold your righteous cause:
> Who against them hath not spoken?
>   They are, just as Jesus was,
>   Persecuted
> By bad men and wicked laws.
>
> Rouse them from their silken slumbers,
>   Trouble them amidst their pride;
> Swell your ranks, augment your numbers,
>   Spread the Charter far and wide:
>   Truth is with us,
> God himself is on our side.[29]

There is a prophetic quality in this hymn that resembles the psalms, but it also identifies God with a particular cause, the People's Char-

---

The way we are likely to interpret hymns like this may not be their authors' intentions, however. Wallace, *Mrs. Alexander*, 70, argues that if you pay attention to the punctuation and read with an emphasis on *God* and *or*, these lines may be "a reproof from Fanny [Alexander] to those of her day who thought the poor somehow less worthy than themselves or made of different clay."

[29] E. P. Thompson, *English Working Class*, 399.

ter of 1838 and the social reforms on behalf of working people associated with it. That justice attended this movement cannot be questioned, but injustice was there too, since both justice and injustice attend all movements and all human activities. The justice of God, which humans are called to do and which the psalms express, always transcends individual movements and, in so doing, turns out to be the most radical of all.

Does the danger here look something like this: does one lose the very justice one rightly seeks by identifying God with the cause of the moment; is the result idolatrous, no matter how well-intentioned? Or, said another way, can you take justice out of the Christian mix and retain it? If you take it out to use by itself without the rest and for a particular cause, do you lose it? We are back here to the general sense of justice in hymnody being more prophetic than the particular.[30]

The Practical Reality

This leads to considering the practical reality of a proposal like Spencer's. Spencer realizes that you can't just replace a people's whole hymnic repertoire with a new one. He says,

> Of course, this radical step is at present an impracticality, if not an impossibility. The black Christian populace seems too entrenched in tradition, too attached to the old "songs of Zion," suddenly to accept more compelling Afrocentric expressions of self-identity and self-determination.[31]

No group will suddenly abandon its memory, not only because that's impossible if a people's being is to remain intact but because its memory contains what is worth keeping. The community sorts out its inheritance over time and abandons what is not worth keeping, content out of step with its faith and texts and music that are poorly crafted and don't sing well. What is worth keeping is not some individual decision by any one person or even several people.

---

[30] There is an interesting parallel here with art. Davie, *Eighteenth Century Hymn in England*, 41, articulates it well when he says, "The nearer art comes to 'the particulars,' the more it is prey to the contingent, including the historically contingent."

[31] Spencer, *Black Hymnody*, 201.

At some times and places strong individuals may exert mighty influences, but even they cannot control everything; the Christian community eventually overrides them, and over time many people are involved in the communal sorting process.

This practical reality is not just a sociological point. It is related to a far more profound theological center. If I understand him, Spencer seems to express an overriding ethnic perspective that is willing to accept the Christian message as a subtheme whenever it is helpful. The "black Christian populace," which he sees as entrenched in tradition, based on observing what they do in their worship services, would appear to stand closer to Martin Luther King., Jr., or Melva Costen[32] and to reverse his categories. They seem to express an overriding Christian perspective and the more radical liberation of all people as an implication. If this analysis is right, one can expect the resistance Spencer suggests, based not only on a sociological inertia but on a different faith. Are there historical parallels to this, some more serious than others: in the church's resistance to Rauschenbusch when it appeared he subordinated Christianity to the Social Gospel, or to Chartism when it appeared to subordinate Christianity to a Charter, or to Nazism when it subordinated the cross to the swastika, or to movements in our period that subordinate Christianity to controlling people by "targeting" them and then using the word "evangelism" as the euphemism for this tyranny, or to the opposite pole of political correctness that seeks to paraphrase all hymns for the sake of whatever the cause of the moment may be?

Since Spencer sees how impractical his proposal is, he suggests this:

> A far less extreme, then, would be to omit or modify hymns containing negative racist and sexist language and imagery, as the more modern black hymnals have done, slowly but surely, since the Civil Rights movement began.[33]

Spencer's suggestion is made as if it were the only, and an unfortunate, option. But, at least from a Christian perspective, is it as unfortunate as he implies? Does the message of the Christian gospel slowly but surely press the church toward a vernacular that is just and toward actions that are just? Is jettisoning what does not express the faith and

---

[32] Costen, *African American Christian Worship.*
[33] Ibid., 201.

casting our language into a more just vernacular doing anything different from what the church has been doing for two thousand years, namely, struggling to work out the implications of a message it never quite grasps but that grasps us, leads us forward, and always subverts our ingrown and self-centered tendencies in spite of ourselves?

We need to be clear that the ingrowness of the church is not only subverted by its quiet ongoing work of liturgical and hymnic singing, revising, and getting the message as clear as possible. Sometimes the church gives weak voice to justice and appears to be an empty shell, and, worse, sometimes the church tries to forget about justice or to remove any concern about it or to subvert it in liturgy turned to antiliturgical death. Then prophetic wake-up calls are in order, sorely needed, and inevitable. The church always has to give thanks for the proposals of Rauschenbusch, Wren, and Spencer—and of Quakers who do not even sing hymns but led charges against slavery and for women's rights. It needs to give thanks for movements for justice that arise in the world when it is asleep and failing its mission. These help rouse the church from its lethargy and disobedience. To have the most prophetic impact, however, they have to flow into and refresh the catholic whole. If they become separate sectarian streams, they dry up.

Does any of this suggest there is measurable progress toward justice in the church or the world? Who knows?[34] With each stride against racism, new strains develop. With each move against sexism, a new glass ceiling closes in. With each attempt to liberate children, new tyrannies appear.[35] The disparity between the rich and the poor increases. Massacres and civil warfare seem endless. Homophobia seems as intractable as racism. Maybe all you do is push evil around a bit, as I've heard Gabriel Fackre say. Maybe each good is accompanied by an equal increase in evil, as I've heard Gary Simpson say. What the church knows is that in the mercy of Christ the battle for justice is ultimately won, and therefore it has no choice but to sing about and do justice now. That means progress is irrelevant as far as impelling us is concerned.

---

[34] See Bright, *Kingdom of God,* 69, where he points to the "Utopian dream . . . will-o'-the-wisp" nature of the hope of peace and at the same time the judgment under which the unrighteous society stands.

[35] See, for example, Smolenski, "Sex Tourism and the Sexual Exploitation of Children," 1079–81.

Wherever there is injustice, the church must attack it whether it is "successful" or not. Because it knows the end of the story as presence and power for our moment from the eschatological moment, it lives and does. And its perspective is therefore the most radical of all, because it never gets tired even if it falls, fails, disagrees, or does evil. The power and presence of God with forgiveness and fresh resources are always there again and again to drive it back into the fray and to make questions of any merit for us in the doing of justice as irrelevant as questions of progress.

As Martin Luther King, Jr., said, precisely in the spirit of the psalms,

> There's something wrong with any church that limits the gospel to talkin' about heaven over yonder. There is something wrong with any minister[s] . . . who become so otherworldly in [their] orientation[s] that [they] forget about what is happening now. There is something wrong with any church that is [so] absolved in the hereafter that it forgets the here. *Here* where men [and women] are trampled over by the iron feet of oppression. *Here* where thousands of God's children are caught in the air-tight cage [of poverty]. *Here* where thousands of men and women are depressed and in agony because of their earthly fight . . . , where the darkness of life surrounds so many of God's children. I say to you that religion must be concerned not merely about mansions in the sky, but about the slums and the ghettos in this world. A proper religion will be concerned not merely about the streets flowing with milk and honey, but about the millions of God's children in Asia, Africa, and South America and in our nation who go to bed hungry at night. It will be concerned [not only] about a long white robe over yonder but about [people] having some clothes down here. It will be concerned not merely about silver slippers in heaven but about men and women having some shoes to wear on earth.[36]

Justice is not the only thing we sing about as Christians, but because we sing about this curious God in Christ who rescues all of us wounded and poverty-stricken folk, we sing about that too—unless, of course, we pervert our own being and the message that brings us into being.

Justice sings because the gospel sings. If we don't sing it, the rocks will cry out.

---

[36] Martin Luther King, Jr., Sermon preached at Ebenezer Baptist Church, Atlanta, July 7, 1963, quoted in Frederick Trost, *Confessing Christ Newsletter*, DeForest, Wisconsin (May 18, 1995).

Bibliography

Augustine. *City of God.* Baltimore: Penguin Books, 1972.

Avila, Rafael. *Worship and Politics.* Maryknoll: Orbis Books, 1981.

Balasuriya, Tissa. *The Eucharist and Human Liberation.* Maryknoll: Orbis Books, 1979.

The Baptist Hymnal. Nashville: Convention Press, 1991.

Bell, John, and Graham Maule. *Heaven Shall Not Wait.* Chicago: GIA Publications, 1989.

_____. *Enemy of Apathy.* Chicago: GIA Publications, 1990.

_____. *Love from Below.* Chicago: GIA Publications, 1989.

Berger, Teresa. *Theology in Hymns? A Study of the Relationship of Doxology and Theology According to* A Collection of Hymns for the Use of the People Called Methodists *(1780).* Trans. Timothy E. Kimbrough. Nashville: Kingswood Books, 1995.

Bishop, Selma L. *Isaac Watts: Hymns and Spiritual Songs, 1707–1748.* London: The Faith Street Press, 1962.

Bonhoeffer, Dietrich. *Life Together.* Trans. John W. Doberstein. New York: Harper & Brothers, 1954.

The Book of Common Prayer . . . According to the Use of The Episcopal Church. New York: The Church Hymnal Corporation, 1979.

Book of Common Worship. Prepared by the Theology and Worship Unit for the Presbyterian Church (U.S.A.) and the Cumberland Presbyterian Church. Louisville: Westminster/John Knox Press, 1993.

Book of Worship United Church of Christ. New York: United Church of Christ Office for Church Life and Leadership, 1986.

[Bread for the Journey]. *Sing a New Song.*

Bright, John. *The Kingdom of God.* Nashville: Abingdon Press, 1953.

Brueggemann Walter. *Israel's Praise: Doxology Against Idolatry and Ideology.* Philadelphia: Fortress Press, 1988.

Brunner, Peter. *Worship in the Name of Jesus.* Trans. M. H. Bertram. St. Louis: Concordia Publishing House, 1968.

Buttrick, George Arthur, ed. *The Interpreter's Dictionary of the Bible*. New York: Abingdon Press, 1962.

Campbell, Will D. *Brother to a Dragonfly*. New York: The Seabury Press, 1977.

Coffin, Henry Sloane, and Ambrose White Vernon, eds. *Hymns for the Kingdom of God*. New York: The A. S. Barnes Co., 1910.

The Collection of Psalms and Hymns. Charles-Town: Lewis Timothy, 1737. Repr. Nashville: The Parthenon Press, n. d.

Costen, Melva Wilson. *African American Christian Worship*. Nashville: Abingdon Press, 1993.

Davie, Donald. *The Eighteenth Century Hymn in England*. Cambridge: Cambridge University Press, 1993.

Dawn, Marva. *Reaching Out Without Dumbing Down: A Theology of Worship for the Turn-of-the-Century Culture*. Grand Rapids: William B. Eerdmans Publishing Co., 1995.

Day, Thomas. *Why Catholics Can't Sing*. New York: Crossroad, 1991.

Doran, Carol Ann. "Metrical Psalmody." *Hymnal Companion to the Lutheran Book of Worship*. Ed. Marilyn Kay Stulken. Philadelphia: Fortress Press, 1981.

Dudley Smith, Timothy. "Charles Wesley—A Hymnwriter for Today." *The Hymn* 39:4 (October 1988) 7–15.

Duffy, Regis. "Symbols of Abundance, Symbols of Need." *Liturgy and Social Justice*. Ed. Mark Searle. Collegeville: The Liturgical Press, 1980.

Durnbaugh, Hedwig T. *German Hymnody of the Brethren, 1720–1903*. Philadelphia: Brethren Encyclopedia, Inc., 1986.

Egan, John J. *Liturgy and Justice*. Collegeville: The Liturgical Press, 1983.

Empereur, James L., and Christopher G. Kiesling. *The Liturgy That Does Justice*. Collegeville: The Liturgical Press, 1990.

The English Hymnal with Tunes. London: Oxford University Press, 1933. 1st ed., 1906.

The [Episcopal] Hymnal 1982. New York: The Church Hymnal Corporation, 1985.

Eskew, Harry, and Hugh T. McElrath. *Sing with Understanding: An Introduction to Christian Hymnology*. Nashville: Church Street Press, 1995.

Fackre, Gabriel. *The Christian Story: A Narrative Interpretation of Basic Christian Doctrine*. Vol. 1. 3d ed. Grand Rapids: William B. Eerdmans Publishing Co., 1996.

____. "Ways of Inclusivity—the Language Debate." *Prism* 9:1 (Spring 1994) 52–65.

Faulkner, Quentin. *Wiser Than Despair*. Westport: Greenwood Press, 1996.

Gaeberlein, Frank E. *The Christian, The Arts, and Truth*. Portland: Multnomah Press, 1985.

Garside, Charles, Jr. *Zwingli and the Arts*. New Haven: Yale University Press, 1966.

Genovese, Eugene D. *Roll, Jordan, Roll*. New York: Vintage Books, 1974.

Gill, Frederick C. *Charles Wesley, the First Methodist.* New York: Abingdon Press, 1964.

Griffin, John Howard. *Black Like Me.* New York: The New American Library of World Literature, 1960.

Halter, Carl, and Carl Schalk, eds. *A Handbook of Church Music.* St. Louis: Concordia Publishing House, 1978.

Hanslick, Eduard. *The Beautiful in Music.* Trans. Gustav Cohen. Indianapolis: The Bobbs-Merrill Company, 1957. First published in 1854 as *Vom Musikalisch-Schoenen.*

Henderson, Frank, and others. *Liturgy, Justice, and the Reign of God: Integrating Vision and Practice.* New York: Paulist Press, 1989.

Hildebrandt, Franz, and others, eds. *The Works of John Wesley, Volume 7: A Collection of Hymns for the Use of the People Called Methodists.* Oxford: Clarendon Press, 1983.

Hilkert, Mary Catherine. *Naming Grace: Preaching and the Sacramental Imagination.* New York: Continuum, 1997.

Hughes, Kathleen, and Mark R. Francis, eds. *Living No Longer for Ourselves: Liturgy and Justice in the Nineties.* Collegeville: The Liturgical Press, 1991.

Hymnal, A Worship Book, Prepared by Churches in the Believers Church Tradition. Elgin: Brethren Press, 1992.

Hymnal of the Protestant Episcopal Church in the United States of America 1940. New York: The Church Pension Fund, 1943.

Hymns on the Lord's Supper . . . With a Preface concerning the Christian Sacrament and Sacrifice, extracted from Doctor Brevint. Bristol: Farley, 1745. Republished in J. Ernest Rattenbury. *The Eucharistic Hymns of John and Charles Wesley.* London: The Epworth Press, 1948.

Hymns Selected and Original . . . for the Evangelical Lutheran Church. Baltimore: Evangelical Lutheran Church, 1847.

Irwin, M. Eleanor. "Phos Hilaron: the Metamorphoses of a Greek Hymn." *The Hymn* 40:2 (April, 1989) 7–12.

Julian, John. *A Dictionary of Hymnology.* New York: Dover Publications, 1957, Repr. of 2d rev. ed. 2 vols., 1907.

Kavanagh, Aidan. *Elements of Rite.* New York: Pueblo Publishing Co., 1982.

Kimbrough, S. T., Jr. *A Song for the Poor: Hymns by Charles Wesley.* New York: Mission Education and Cultivation Program Department of the General Board of Global Ministries, The United Methodist Church, 1993.

King, Martin Luther, Jr. *Letter from Birmingham Jail.* 1963.

____. Sermon preached at Ebenezer Baptist Church, Atlanta, July 7, 1963. *Confessing Christ Newsletter.* DeForest, Wis. (May 18, 1995).

Lamb, John Alexander. *The Psalms in Christian Worship.* London: The Faith Press, 1962.

Langer, Susanne K. *Feeling and Form.* New York: Charles Scribner's Sons, 1953.

____. *Philosophy in a New Key: A Study in the Symbolism of Reason, Rite, and Art.* Cambridge: Harvard University Press, 1942.

Lathrop, Gordon ed. "What Are the Ethical Implications of Worship?" *Open Questions in Worship* 6. Minneapolis: Augsburg Fortress, 1996.

Lawson, Mary Sackville, ed. *Collected Hymns, Sequences, and Carols of John Mason Neale.* London: Hodder & Stoughton, 1914.

Lead Me, Guide Me: The African American Catholic Hymnal. Chicago: GIA Publications, 1987.

Leaver, Robin. *Come to the Feast: The Original and Translated Hymns of Martin Franzmann.* St. Louis: Concordia Publishing House, 1994.

Leupold, Ulrich S. ed. *Luther's Works, Volume 53, Liturgy and Hymns.* Philadelphia: Fortress Press, 1965.

Lewis, C. S. *Christian Reflections.* Ed. Walter Hooper. Grand Rapids: William B. Eerdmans Publishing Co., 1967.

Lutheran Book of Worship. Minneapolis: Augsburg Publishing House, 1978.

Lutheran Book of Worship: Minister's Desk Edition. Minneapolis: Augsburg Publishing House, 1978.

Macleod, George. *Only One Way Left: Church Prospect.* Glasgow: The Iona Community, 1956.

Marissen, Michael. *The Social and Religious Designs of J. S. Bach's Brandenberg Concertos.* Princeton: Princeton University Press, 1995.

Marshall, Madeleine Forell. *Common Hymnsense.* Chicago: GIA Publications, 1995.

_____. "'The Holy Ghost Is Amorous in His Metaphors': The Divine Love Hymn Reclaimed." *Cross Accent* 5A:9 (January 1997) 17–23.

McKinnon, James. *Music in Early Christian Literature.* Cambridge: Cambridge University Press, 1987.

Mead, Sidney E. *The Lively Experiment: The Shaping of Christianity in America.* New York: Harper & Row, 1963.

Meyer, Leonard B. *Emotion and Meaning in Music.* Chicago: University of Chicago Press, 1956.

Meyer, Lester. "A Lack of Laments in the Church's Use of the Psalter." *Lutheran Quarterly* 7:1 (Spring 1993) 67–78.

Migne, J. P. *Patrologiae Cursus Completus, Series Prima, XVI, S.Ambrosii.* Paris, 1845.

Miller, Patrick D., Jr. "The Psalms as Praise and Poetry." *The Hymn* 40:4 (October 1989) 12–16.

Muhlenberg, Henry Melchior. *The Journals of Henry Melchior Muhlenberg In Three Volumes.* Trans. Theodore G. Tappert and John W. Doberstein. Philadelphia: The Muhlenberg Press, 1942.

Mussey, Mabel Hay Barrows, ed. *Social Hymns of Brotherhood and Aspiration.* New York: The A. S. Barnes Co., 1914.

Neale, John Mason. *Songs and Ballads for Manufacturers.* 2d ed. London, 1850.

Nevin, W. W. *Dies Irae, Nine Original Versions.* New York: G. P. Putnam Sons, 1895.

The New Century Hymnal. Cleveland: The Pilgrim Press, 1995.

114

Niebuhr, H. Richard. *Christ and Culture*. New York: Harper & Row, 1951.

Niebuhr, Reinhold. "Sects and Churches." *The Christian Century* 52:27 (July 3, 1935) 885–87.

The Orthodox Liturgy. London: Society for Promoting Christian Knowledge, 1939.

Peters, Erskine. *Lyrics of the Afro-American Spiritual*. Westport: Greenwood Press, 1993.

Polack, W. G. *The Handbook to the Lutheran Hymnal*. St. Louis: Concordia Publishing House, 1942.

Porter, Thomas C. "English Versions of the Dies Irae." *Reformed Church Review* 5:1 (January 1901) 24–32.

Praying Together: English Language Liturgical Consultation. Abingdon Press, 1988.

The Presbyterian Hymnal. Louisville: Westminster/John Knox Press, 1990.

Psalms and Hymns for the Use of the German Reformed Church in the United States of America. Chambersburg: Publication Office of the German Reformed Church, 1845.

Raboteau, Albert J. *Slave Religion: The 'Invisible Institution' in the Antebellum South*. New York: Oxford University Press, 1978.

Ramshaw, Gail. *God Beyond Gender: Feminist Christian God-Language*. Minneapolis: Fortress Press, 1995.

____. "The Place of Lament Within Praise: Theses for Discussion." *Worship* 61:4 (July 1987) 317–22.

Rattenbury, J. Ernest. *The Eucharistic Hymns of John and Charles Wesley*. London: The Epworth Press, 1948.

Rauschenbusch, Walter, and Ira D. Sankey, eds. *Evangeliums-Lieder, Gospel Hymns mit deutschen Kernliedern*. New York: The Biglow & Main Co., 1890.

Rejoice in the Lord. Grand Rapids: Wm. B. Eerdmans Publishing Co., 1985.

Routley, Erik. *Church Music and the Christian Faith*. Carol Stream: Agape, 1978.

____. *A Panorama of Christian Hymnody*. Collegeville: The Liturgical Press, 1979.

____. *A Short History of English Church Music*. Carol Stream: Hope Publishing Co., 1997.

Saliers, Don E. *Worship as Theology: Foretaste of Glory Divine*. Nashville: Abingdon Press, 1994.

Sankey, Ira, and others. *Gospel Hymns Nos. 1 to 6 Complete*. New York: Da Capo Press, 1972. Reprint of "Excelsior Edition" of 1895.

Schalk, Carl. *God's Song in a New Land: Lutheran Hymnals in America*. St. Louis: Concordia Publishing House, 1995.

Schattauer, Thomas. "The Church Year." *Parish Education Series: Study Guides Relating to Music and Worship*. Ed. Paul Westermeyer. St. Louis: Morning Star, 1992.

Searle, Mark, ed. *Liturgy and Social Justice.* Collegeville: The Liturgical Press, 1980.

Sedgwick, Timothy F. *Sacramental Ethics: Paschal Identity and the Christian Life.* Philadelphia: Fortress Press, 1987.

Senn, Frank C. "'Worship Alive': An Analysis and Critique of 'Alternative Worship Services.'" *Worship* 69:3 (May 1995) 194–223.

Service Book and Hymnal of the Lutheran Church in America. Minneapolis: Augsburg Publishing House, 1958.

Sessions, Roger. *Questions About Music.* New York: W. W. Norton & Co., 1971.

Shriver, Donald W. *An Ethic for Enemies.* New York: Oxford University Press, 1995.

Sing a New Song. Light brown; n.d., n.p.

Sizer, Sandra S. *Gospel Hymns and Social Religion: The Rhetoric of Nineteenth-Century Revivalism.* Philadelphia: Temple University Press, 1978.

Smith, Harmon. *Where Two or Three Are Gathered: Liturgy and the Moral Life.* Cleveland: The Pilgrim Press, 1995.

Smolenski, Carol. "Sex Tourism and the Sexual Exploitation of Children." *The Christian Century* 112:33 (November 15, 1995) 1079–81.

Spencer, Jon Michael. *Black Hymnody: A Hymnological History of the African-American Church.* Knoxville: University of Tennessee Press, 1992.

_____. "Hymns of the Social Awakening: Walter Rauschenbusch and Social Gospel Hymnody." *The Hymn* 40:2 (April 1989) 18–24.

_____. *Sing a New Song: Liberating Black Hymnody.* Minneapolis: Fortress Press, 1995.

Stamps, Mary E. ed. *To Do Justice and Right Upon the Earth: Papers from the Virgil Michel Symposium on Liturgy and Social Justice.* Collegeville: The Liturgical Press, 1983.

Stravinsky, Igor. *An Autobiography.* New York: W. W. Norton & Co., 1936.

Stringfellow, William. *Free in Obedience.* New York: The Seabury Press, 1964.

_____. *My People Is the Enemy: An Autobiographical Polemic.* New York: Holt, Rinehart & Winston, 1964.

_____. *A Private and Public Faith.* Grand Rapids: William B. Eerdmans Publishing Co., 1962.

Tate, N., and N. Brady, eds. *A New Version of the Psalms of David.* Boston: Joshua Belcher, 1813.

Terrien, Samuel. *The Magnificat: Musicians as Biblical Interpreters.* New York: Paulist Press, 1995.

Thompson, Bard. *Liturgies of the Western Church.* Cleveland: Meridian Books, 1961.

Thompson, E. P. *The Making of the English Working Class.* New York: Vintage Books, 1963.

Tillich, Paul. *Love, Power, and Justice: Ontological Analyses and Ethical Applications.* New York: Oxford University Press, 1960.

Troeger, Thomas. *Borrowed Light: Hymn Texts, Prayers, and Poems.* New York: Oxford University Press, 1994.

Tucker, Karen Westerfield. "Liturgical Expressions of Care for the Poor in the Wesleyan Tradition: A Case Study for the Ecumenical Church," *Worship* 69:1 (January 1995) 51–64.

The United Methodist Book of Worship. Nashville: The United Methodist Publishing House, 1992.

The United Methodist Hymnal. Nashville: The United Methodist Publishing Co., 1989.

Vollstaendiges Marburger Gesangbuch. Germantown: Christoph Saur, 1757.

Walker, Wyatt Tee. *"Somebody's Calling My Name," Black Sacred Music and Social Change.* Valley Forge: Judson Press, 1992. 1st printing, 1979.

Wallace, Valerie. *Mrs. Alexander: A Life of the Hymn-Writer.* Dublin: The Lilliput Press, 1995.

Walton, Janet R. *Art and Worship: A Vital Connection.* Collegeville: The Liturgical Press, 1991.

Watts, I. *The Psalms of David Imitated in the Language of the New Testament And Applied to the Christian State and Worship.* Boston: Mein & Fleeming, 1768.

Westermeyer, Paul. *With Tongues of Fire.* St. Louis: Concordia Publishing House, 1995.

_____. "The Hymnal Noted: Theological and Musical Intersections." *Church Music* 73:2. 1–9.

_____. "Sharper Than Any Two-Edged Sword." *Liturgy* 11:1 (Summer 1993) 51–57.

_____. "To Be Human Is to Sing." *The Luther Northwestern Story* 7:1 (Winter 1990) 4–8.

White, James F. *Sacraments as God's Self Giving: Sacramental Practice and Faith.* Nashville: Abingdon Press, 1983.

_____. "Introduction." *The Sunday Service of the Methodists in North America.* The United Methodist Publishing House, 1984.

_____. "Worship as a Source of Injustice." *Reformed Liturgy and Music* 19:2 (Spring 1985) 72–76.

White, R. E. O. *A Christian Handbook to the Psalms.* Grand Rapids: William B. Eerdmans Publishing Co., 1984.

Wiesel, Elie. *Night.* Trans. Rodway and others. Hill & Wang, 1960.

Willimon, William H. *The Service of God: How Worship and Ethics Are Related.* Nashville: Abingdon Press, 1983.

Winkworth, Catherine. *The Chorale Book for England.* London: Longman, Green, Longman, Roberts, & Green, 1963.

With One Voice. Minneapolis: Augsburg Fortress, 1995.

Wolterstorff, Nicholas. *Art in Action: Toward a Christian Aesthetic.* Grand Rapids: William B. Eerdmans Publishing Co., 1980.

_____. *Until Justice and Peace Embrace.* Grand Rapids: William B. Eerdmans Publishing Co., 1983.

WITHDRAWN

____. "Why Care About Justice?" *Evangelicalism: Surviving Its Success.* Pp. 156–167. Ed. David A. Fraser. Princeton: Princeton University Press, 1987.

Worship Third Edition: A Hymnal and Service Book for Roman Catholics. Chicago: GIA Publications, 1986.

Wren, Brian. *Education for Justice.* London: SCM Press, 1989.

____. *Faith Looking Forward.* Carol Stream: Hope Publishing Co., 1983.

____. *Piece Together Praise.* Carol Stream: Hope Publishing Co., 1996.

____. *What Language Shall I Borrow? God-Talk in Worship: A Male Response to Feminist Theology.* New York: Crossroad, 1989.

Young, Carlton R. *Music of the Heart: John and Charles Wesley on Church Music and Musicians.* Carol Stream: Hope Publishing Co., 1995.

Young, Carlton R. "The New Century Hymnal, 1995." *The Hymn* 48:2 (April 1997) 25–38.